The Mirror of Zen

The Mirror of Zen

The Classic Guide to Buddhist Practice
by Zen Master So Sahn

Translated from the Chinese by
Boep Joeng

Translated from the Korean by
Hyon Gak

Shambhala
Boston & London
2006

Shambhala Publications, Inc.
Horticultural Hall
300 Massachusetts Avenue
Boston, Massachusetts 02115
www.shambhala.com

9 8 7 6 5 4 3 2 1
First Edition
Printed in the United States of America

⊛ This edition is printed on acid-free paper that meets the American National Standards Institute Z39.48 Standard.

Distributed in the United States by Random House, Inc.,
and in Canada by Random House of Canada Ltd

Interior design and composition: Greta D. Sibley & Associates

Library of Congress Cataloging-in-Publication Data
Sŏsan Taesa, 1520–1604.
[Sŏn'ga kwigam. English]
The mirror of zen: the classic guide to Buddhist practice by zen master So Sahn/translation from Chinese to Korean by Boep Joeng: translated from Korean to English by Hyon Gak.
p. cm.
ISBN-13: 978-1-59030-384-9 (pbk.: alk. paper)
ISBN-10: 1-59030-384-9
1. Zen Buddhism—Early works to 1800. I. Pŏpchong. II. Hyŏn'gak, 1964– . III. Title.
BQ9265.S66713 2006
294.3'927—dc22
2006014804

Contents

Preface to the English Edition

The present translation of *The Mirror of Zen* is the first complete version of this timeless classic to appear in English in the West.

If you were to comb the mountains and valleys of Korea, polling every meditating monk and nun and hermit and ascetic as to the most necessary, essential, inseparable compendium of teachings apart from the Buddha's sutras themselves, chances are that most of them would choose *The Mirror of Zen*. It is by far the most quoted, most cited, most referred-to text in the tea rooms and teaching halls of the Zen temples in Korea. Nuns and monks will often have an old master write one of its famous verses in flowing calligraphy, to paste on the wall of their ascetic hut, or to give to a fellow meditator as a precious gift to spur their practice. Like every Korean monk and nun, my own teacher, Zen Master Seung Sahn, was deeply influenced by Master So Sahn's teachings: the exhortations and stories from this text abound in his talks. And when Zen Master Seung Sahn arrived in America, one of the first things he attempted to accomplish was to encourage one of his close students to translate this work. (It was never completed.) His own book, *The Compass of Zen*, is a direct, even conscious spiritual descendant of *The Mirror of Zen*, explicitly sharing both its intent, compactness, and even structure. For centuries, *The Mirror of Zen* has been used in Japanese and Chinese Zen halls by adepts who have come to learn of its pithy directives to practice.

Being neither a scholar nor a professional translator, I would never in my right mind have had the audacity to so finger such a venerated text. The undertaking was urged, instead, with great gentle force by the Venerable Boep Joeng, a Zen monk, activist, poet, and by all accounts the most revered living spiritual figure in any religion in modern-day South Korea. His own version of *The Mirror of Zen*, translated several decades ago from classical Chinese into vernacular Korean, had recently been selected by the Korean government to represent prominent works of Korean arts and letters at the Frankfurt Book Fair in Germany. His own translation is regarded as the best rendering from Chinese into a vernacular language, and my translation "looks through the eyes" of his own translation to bring *The Mirror of Zen* into English.

So, for the record, those with more training in the field of Chinese or Buddhist classics might need to know how someone with no scholarly preparation in the field came to translate a work of such a stature as *The Mirror of Zen*.

One day in March 2004, I was told that Venerable Boep Joeng Sunim requested a meeting at Gil Sang Sah, a temple in north central Seoul. At the time I was the guiding teacher of the Seoul International Zen Center at Hwa Gye Sah Temple, and secretary attending upon my teacher, Zen Master Seung Sahn. Would I be able to translate this work into English, to help introduce it to the world?

Complain though I may of my ignorance of Chinese characters, and a competing inadequacy in written, much less literary, Korean, Boep Joeng Sunim would have nothing of it. Just kneeling in the presence of this great monk, or having any kind of audience with him, is a singularly rare experience. He stubbornly refuses frequent visits to the city, preferring instead his rundown shack located nowhere in the mountains. He has also adamantly refused to permit his own writings to be translated into English, perhaps because he knows it would bring increased international renown into his austere spiritual life.

With his main student quietly serving delicately scented green tea beside us, it was unimaginably difficult to escape this request. The burden of translating Boep Joeng Sunim's voice was one huge imponderable, but looming so vastly behind it, like a great, towering peak poking distantly through the mists of a formidable range, was Master So Sahn himself. And this was his seminal work. And I am just a Zen monk, a New Jersey–born American one at that, blatantly deficient in practice and virtue, and one who hasn't studied a spot of classical Chinese.

As I desperately ticked off the names of several people far more qualified than me to undertake this responsibility, to each one Boep Joeng Sunim only shook his head. His lips pursed tightly as the list lengthened. And it was from this moment that the rationale behind his gentle obstinacy became clear: "Not just anybody can translate this book and get Master So Sahn's true meaning," he said. "The people you mention are not practicing people. Each one of them might be qualified in this way or that with words, and maybe understand English. But they do not practice meditation. Only one who really practices meditation— and even better, a meditation monk, who commits body-and-soul—can touch this teaching's true meaning. And so much better if that monk truly practices correctly."

So, Boep Joeng Sunim's concern has been with meditation— pure and simple—not intellectual preparation. For him, the inner meaning of this work for meditators was supreme, far more so than the scholarly rightness of a conservative, rigid translation. Some six months into the project, after encountering numerous situations wherein I realized that a merely literalistic, word-for-word Chinese-to-Korean-to-English rendering would not only be boring and insufficient, but even miss entirely, on many essential points of teaching, Master So Sahn's subtle and profound meanings, I again approached Boep Joeng Sunim. To which approach should I hew, and still have his confidence in my efforts?

His words in that moment opened up this great text's deeper possibilities, and sent me back to the project with greater confidence: "Of all the sutras translated in China," he said, "there are basically two great masters whose translations from Sanskrit into Chinese are best known to us today. Venerable Hyon Jang translated the sutras word-for-word, very strictly and conservatively adhering to the most literal, 'correct' conversion of each Sanskrit word into its nearest Chinese equivalent. And Venerable Kumarajiva, while translating correctly, allowed a more open reading, permitting the texts to read somewhat differently than an overly literal translation. Some at the time believed his translations were unorthodox, even incorrect. But what was important to Kumarajiva was how well the texts could be conveyed in the Chinese way of expressing things, in a way that was more natural to them than any stricter translation would ever permit. And you know what? It is Kumarajiva's translations that today are more highly esteemed, and definitely favored by more meditation monks than anything that the supposedly 'correct' Venerable Hyon Jang ever produced." After sipping his tea, he closed his eyes and said with a very subtle smile, "Now, you must become an American Kumarajiva!"

Scholars may be disappointed with this appointment, and with justification. But he urged me over and over again to produce a reading that would be comfortable to the way modern Western readers conceive of the sorts of issues that Master So

Sahn raises. I have endeavored at all costs to produce a translation that, while meticulously listening to every Chinese character that Master So Sahn inscribed, is yet not enslaved by the conventional reading of these characters, especially given the fact that he writes in a very formalistic style in an age and monastic setting so inconceivably distant from our own, in the West.

If I have succeeded in any way, then as you read this, you will not meet a distant and moldy ancient, speaking in impenetrable density across the vast stretches of the centuries, but rather a teacher sitting cross-legged right in front of you, speaking in your own language to your own practice as it unfolds in this very moment.

A note on the spellings: The audience for this text is, of course, readers in a Western context. But it is a text that contains stories relating to Indian, Chinese, and Korean teachers, texts, temple and place names, and teachings. Each of these linguistic systems has its own rules for transliterating proper names into English. There is no possible way to standardize the spellings of all proper names and terms that would satisfy the experience of readers in the West, all of whom will come at this text from their own spiritual traditions.

Sanskrit terms remain transliterated in the standard English style. But to "Koreanize" the English transliteration of Chinese Buddhist proper and place names simply for the sake of homogenous "standardization" would be confusing to many Western readers who have long been familiar with names that have been fairly standardized in the English imagination through many years of translation by scholars of Chinese and Japanese.

So, in the case of Chinese and Korean names and terms, a standard Chinese style, Wade-Giles, has been adopted for Chinese names and terms, and a Korean style for Korean names and terms.

Monastic names for senior monks are often four-character arrangements, so in order to set them off visually from each other, the Chinese names are hyphenated, whereas the Korean names, where the four characters are used, are not hyphenated. This gives the reader an instant visual sense of context, of who comes from which tradition, which I believe outweighs any rigidity about any one style.

A translation is, at best, merely a pale reflection of the original. The most competent effort simply holds up a mirror to the original, and, even at its most painstakingly faithful, can do little better than reflect the basic color and shape of the original. Images in mirrors may be correct, but they are never—ever—the complete experience of the original. The texture, the feel, the smell and taste of the original object cannot be expressed by the reflected image.

Such would be true for any work of translation. And yet it is even more so when one is engaged in translating a seminal work of Zen teaching, a work which itself wishes to function as a mirror—not depending on words or speech, pointing directly to our true nature. Attempting any translation of a scriptural work is, at its very origin, fraught with error: how much more so when translating the mirrorlike mind of a great master of Zen. For doesn't Zen Master So Sahn himself say that, while all scriptural teachings use words to point to the realm of the wordless, Zen teaching uses wordlessness to point to the realm of the wordless? So how do you remain perfectly faithful to conveying *that*?

Venerable Boep Joeng Sunim (b. 1932) may not be a household name in the West, but his teachings and—most of all—his life of solitary meditation, strict personal austerity, and extraordinary moral and physical clarity are known to all Koreans. Though his writings are read by all, across religions, and his books have routinely been the best-selling titles for the last thirty or forty years, he eschews wealth, titles, and positions, even his own temple, and instead lives in a rude lean-to shack without running water or electricity, deep in the mountains in the remotest section of the country. The cabin's location is unknown even to his own monastic disciples. His stringent adherence to a strict moral code of possessionless freedom is legendary.

The translation of Venerable Boep Joeng Sunim's text was the raison d'être for this undertaking. But fundamental to it all is, after all, Master So Sahn's primary text. While of course basing this work squarely on Venerable Boep Joeng Sunim's rendering, I have, at every turn, and *for every single character*, returned to meet Master So Sahn's dense Chinese text directly. I have taken great pains at this because of the chance that Venerable Boep Joeng Sunim's Korean-oriented expressions might even slightly prejudice the primary meaning away from how we would express—and receive it—in English. To further insulate this work from the contamination of my own ignorance, I often consulted the translation by another great modern monk, Master Song Dahm, in the case of variant meanings. I have consulted with other monks regarding areas where my knowledge of Chinese or Buddhism was particularly weak. They shall not be mentioned here, for fear of including them in my guilt in this work's obvious deficiencies.

And I conducted this translation over a two-and-a-half-year period, all the while putting the work down every three months to participate in the traditional three-month intensive silent meditation retreats, which have been my life's devotion for the last sixteen years. At the end of three months, returning from the misty mountains, the *Mirror* always awaited, and I could pick it up, fresh from ninety days of nothing but intensive meditation, to gaze into its meanings—and my English renderings of them—anew. While this sort of schedule certainly lengthened the time it has taken to complete this holy burden, it is also my solemn wish that a period spent sharing this work with an ever deeper commitment to the meditative life has given the translation a lived depth, some freshness, some grounding in the life that Master So Sahn is pointing to, and especially, some authenticity.

I would like to acknowledge the assistance of Ms. Sohn Jong-In, who provided for me a rough preliminary sketch of the manuscript. I have also been guided by an in-house unpublished translation of *The Mirror of Zen* done several years ago by my good friend, Charles Mark Mueller, for the Chogye Order of Korean Buddhism. It was that initial translation that first opened Master So Sahn's world to me, and I thank him for his efforts, as well as for generously contributing his thoughts at various points of this manuscript.

Grateful acknowledgment to everyone at Shambhala Publications, especially Jonathan Green, Eden Steinberg, and Ben Gleason for their appreciation of this work and their extraordinarily delicate professionalism in all aspects of its production.

> First Day of the Three-Month Winter
> Meditation Intensive, 2006
> The Zen Hall in Joeng Hae Sah, at Su Dok
> Sah Temple, Dok Seung Sahn Mountain,
> Republic of Korea
>
> Hyon Gak Sunim

Preface to the Korean Edition

BOEP JOENG SUNIM

The Mirror of Zen was written by the Great Master So Sahn Hyu Jeong. As stated in the introduction, written by the Great Master himself, as well as in the epilogue, written by his disciple, the Venerable Sam Yong, this book is not entirely the creation of the Great Master. He selected the essence of the Buddha's teachings from more than fifty volumes of sutras and *dharma-shastras*, as well as from teachings and anecdotes of the Patriarchs. At first he only wrote down the original words right out of these primary sources. But years later he added commentaries, short *gathas*, and capping words to the original material in order to help his disciples who had difficulty in understanding the core teachings.

Through *The Mirror of Zen* we can catch a glimpse of the situation in which the Zen School and the Sutra School often differed with each other's teaching and practicing styles in a Korea of some four hundred years ago. The Great Master spoke of his own view on Zen and the sutras as follows:

Zen is the Buddha's mind, while the sutras are the Buddha's words.
Shakyamuni Buddha is the source of both the Zen meditation and Sutra traditions, whereas the distinction in practice between the two traditions begins with Venerable

Mahakashyapa and Venerable Ananda, respectively. Zen meditation employs the wordless to reveal what is beyond words, whereas the sutras rely on words to express what is beyond words. So mind itself is the Zen teaching, and speech is the sutra teaching. Dharma has but one taste, yet the difference between realizing it and merely understanding it—conceptually—is as vast as that between heaven and earth.

He thus made it clear that the practice of Zen and the practice of the sutras are not two but one. Yet at the same time he clearly advocated the priority of enlightenment experience, and in so doing implicitly granted the superiority of Zen as embodying the most essential teaching of Buddhism.

In addition, Master So Sahn clarifies his own view of the Pure Land School, since this tradition's practice of calling out to Amita Buddha was simply ignored or even disdained by many members of the Zen School at the time. Taking on another delicate criticism of so-called "orthodox Zen," he reemphasizes the role of precepts study. This was done not in a schoolmarmish sort of approach to reining in meditation practitioners, but rather for the purpose of awakening those pseudo-Zen monks who claimed that nothing—not even the precepts—matters but enlightenment.

As a result of his efforts, this deceptively slim and concise text deserves to be regarded not only as the mirror of Zen but also as the universal mirror of Buddhist study as a whole. Its main audience is, of course, practitioners who have entered the Buddhist monastic life. But it also opens the sure path to a life of wisdom for laity who wish to live with a clear and compassionate mind.

The author is commonly known as Great Master So Sahn, since he spent most of his life at Mount Myo Hyang, in present-day North Korea. One of the traditional names for this great mountain was So Sahn ("Western Mountain"), and there were many great temples there, with many hundreds of monks engaged in deep meditation practice. As a pen name, he called himself Baek Hwa Do, in remembrance of the temple where he did some of his most arduous practice, Baek Hwa Temple in the famed Diamond Mountains. He also called himself Do Eun after he resigned as the Judge of Zen and Doctrinal Schools. His dharma name was Hyu Jeong, and his pen name was Cheong Heo.

He was born on the twenty-sixth of March 1520, in Anju, a city in the Pyong-Ahn Province of what is now modern North Korea. He lost his mother at the age of nine, and lost his father the next year. A country magistrate took in this brilliant orphan with a stunning talent for writing, and eventually saw the young boy enter the highest educational institution of the time in Korea, the Song Kyun Kwan in present-day Seoul, a training ground for Confucian elites founded in 1308. The boy was only twelve years old.

He traveled south to remote Jeolla Province with his teacher, but the teacher soon returned to Seoul upon the death of his parent. Young So Sahn was left behind, and in his isolation, one day he set out on a journey with friends from the village school. During the journey, he first came to learn the Buddhist sutras from the Venerable Sung In at Mount Ji Ri. Seeing the inner road to which the sutras were pointing, he began immediately to practice Zen under the guidance of Zen Master Bu Yong Yong Kwan when he was only eighteen years old. At the age of twenty-one he was awakened, and only then received the precepts to become a monk.

After eight years of continuous study, one day while walking through a village he attained sudden enlightenment at the sound of a cock crowing. He wrote a verse to express his experience:

Didn't they say in the old days
That your mind does not turn gray even though
    your hair does?
In hearing the sound of a cock crowing,
A Great Man's work is fulfilled.

Young So Sahn easily passed the extremely difficult state examination that determined entrance into monastic life, and was soon appointed to be a leader of the Zen School, and then a leader of the Sutra School. After three years in official service, he resigned the posts and returned to the Diamond Mountains to live out a life of solitary meditation.

Meanwhile, a simple poem that Master So Sahn had written happened to give rise to public debate, even suspicion of him being involved in some of the political intrigues of the day. But when he was brought in for questioning before the all-powerful king himself, the court could not help but be moved by the simplicity and radiant compassion in his features. It was immediately clear by his bearing and soft voice that this diminutive monk was involved in no wish for the ways of the world, and he was acquitted forthwith by a special grant from King Seon Jo himself. From that day forth, recognizing in each other a mutual karmic affection, the Master remained on friendly terms with the king for years thereafter.

But then something happened to his country that carved out for Master So Sahn a special role in the protection of the Korean people. It was not a role expected of monks, but one that

Master So Sahn acquitted himself of (however reluctantly, and with pained heart) so majestically that he is one of the most beloved Korean historical figures to this day.

Japan invaded Korea in 1592, and began a bloody march up and down the peninsula, destroying its greatest masterpieces or looting them and sending them off to Japan. The Korean people, long schooled by Confucian mores against the training of a standing army, were absolutely powerless in the face of this onslaught, with barely any fighting force. Marauding invaders moved throughout the cities and countryside with total impunity, its women, innumerable cultural masterpieces, and greatest artisans carted off to Japan. The nation was on the verge of collapse.

Until that time, Confucian leaders had been suppressing Buddhism, which had been the state religion for many centuries, until the rise of Confucian government. But with many thousands of monks confined to vast monasteries, the government had no choice: The highly disciplined training and organization of Buddhist monastic communities provided the only chance for the royal Confucian government—constantly on the run from the tightening noose of Japanese aggression—to mount any kind of effective defense. It was a pool of manpower not to be overlooked.

Confucian leaders appealed to the most influential monk of the time to bring this extraordinary resource to the aid of the nation, but there was little chance of success. How could men schooled in the tenets of compassion and non-harming be convinced to participate in the defense of the nation, the state—a worldly entity admittedly part of the artificial world of samsaric appearances?

Master So Sahn was known as a reconciler of seeming opposites. He had unified the Zen meditation and Sutra schools, despite their deep-rooted differences. Could he reconcile the mortal peril of the nation with a monastic tradition based squarely on teachings that emphasized compassion and non-harming, much less avoiding killing any life?

Approached by court officials in his solitary retirement—some of the very officials charged with carrying out the suppression of Buddhism—Great Master So Sahn reflected deeply on the dilemma. Considering the uniqueness and depth of the Korean Buddhist tradition, he knew that if the nation were to fall, the world would potentially lose a vessel of the Dharma that was greater than merely the loss of a government or a state or even a particular race. He quickly determined that, for the sake of preserving this unique treasure of Dharma that was Korean Buddhism, he had to protect the culture and the nation that had built and sustained it.

At the age of sixty-nine, and with great heaviness hanging in his heart for the unavoidable suffering that would certainly result from his decision, Master So Sahn traveled the length and breadth of the country, raising an army of thousands of monk soldiers in the cause of justice and loyalty. Their discipline and fortitude and dedication to a singular goal were qualities that changed the course of the invasion. The Japanese were overwhelmed at the sight of these legions of Buddhist monks marching through the countryside, defending their country yet committing no atrocities against their invaders. Those attackers who had the good fortune to fall into the hands of Master So Sahn's army were not beheaded or even tortured (as was the minimum custom afforded most prisoners of war in those days), but treated with humanity and compassion. And yet it must be said that the fighting prowess of this "monk army" was up to the power of the Japanese invaders, and even surpassed it in several major battles.

Master So Sahn and his vast monk army were a constant thorn in the side of the Japanese, and contributed greatly to the early withdrawal of Japanese forces from the Korean peninsula. When peace was finally achieved, Master So Sahn was appointed to the highest office of Korean Buddhism. No less historic a figure than the great General Lee Yo-Song, the commander-in-chief of Chinese reinforcements in Korea, paid a tribute to Master So Sahn with these simple words:

> Having renounced fame and honor for the sake of
> practicing the Tao,
> the Great Master came forth for his country in peril.

As soon as Seoul was recaptured and the king returned to the palace, the Great Master resigned again because of old age, and recommended for the post two of his disciples, Venerable Sam Yong and Venerable Cheo Yeong. Shunning royal titles and offers of further worldly power in the newly reconstituted government, he returned to monastic life, traveling like an empty cloud deep in the famed Diamond Mountains, in Mount Ji Ri and Mount Myo Hyang. It is said that he always had more than a thousand disciples in constant attendance, waiting for every word of his teaching, and produced over seventy enlightened dharma successors.

On the twenty-third of January, 1604, the Great Master gave a dharma talk to his disciples gathered together at Won Jeok Sah Temple in Mount Myo Hyang. Then, suddenly glancing at his own portrait hanging on the wall, he stopped speaking and wrote down a poem. After inscribing the final line, he entered nirvana while sitting erect in meditation.

His death poem is as follows:

> Eighty years ago, that was me.
> After eighty years, am I that?

His writings are *The Mirror of Zen, The Understanding of Zen and Doctrines, The Mirror of Three Schools, The Altar of Cloud and Water,* and *Cheong-heo Collections* in four volumes.

The first time I read *The Mirror of Zen* was during an intensive meditation retreat at Do Seol Zen Center in Hae In Sah Temple, when I borrowed a copy of the mimeographed book from an old monk. I found that every word in it was alive, the true "live word" that he urged upon students in his text, a sincere dharma talk accessible to all practitioners of the Way.

These were the days before photocopiers in Korea. So I rushed to the village down below the temple to buy a student notebook, and began to copy the book by hand at night, using a small pencil that I sharpened with a knife. I had copied about half of it when the old monk who had first lent me the book saw that the light was still on in my room late into the night. When I told him what I was doing, he smiled and said, "If you like that book so much, you may keep it." Tears streaming down my face, I bowed deeply to him. I have appreciated his kindness to the very day I write these words.

Since then, I have always wanted to help fellow practitioners to read this book.

In the summer of 1961, I began to translate Master So Sahn's original Chinese-language text into Korean at Hae In Sah Temple. My references were the original edition of *Zen and the Doctrines,* another Chinese edition from Won Jeok Sah Temple, and the Korean edition from Song Gwang Sah Temple. I was even more encouraged by the similarities between past and present: the situation in Korean Buddhism that had prompted the author to write this book four hundred years ago was still very relevant to the situation in Korean Buddhism today.

The first edition of my translation was published in 1962 under the name of Seonhak-ganhaeng-hoe by Boep Tong Sah. The revised edition was published in 1971 by Hong Boep Won, and the publisher was changed to Jeong Um Mun Goh in 1976. This version went into many editions and has been steadily read in and out of Buddhist circles, of course only because Master So Sahn provides such sincere teaching.

Similar Korean editions of this book have recently poured out under the names of various translators and by various publishers. While working on a revision of this edition recently, I felt fortunate enough to have an opportunity to read the original text again. However well we may think we know them, great classics always inspire us afresh whenever we return to them. I also had a chance to correct some mistakes in the previous edition. I would like to express my gratitude to the publisher, Dong Jjok Nara, for the opportunity to compare the old edition with the new one word-by-word, aiming at even greater perfection and clarity.

When studying Buddhist scriptures [sutras], if you do not reflect deeply on your own mind at the same time, you could study the entire 84,000-volume canon of the Buddha's words and still it would not do you any good whatsoever.

These are the words of the Great Master So Sahn himself, and with sincerest gratitude to him I commend them to the practice and, most important, the enlightenment of all who presently hold this holy text.

Kil Sang Sah Temple, Seoul

[Venerable] Boep Joeng Sunim

The Mirror of Zen

Introduction

Those who studied Buddhism in the old days would not speak a word if it had not been the Buddha's word, nor did an action if it had not been the Buddha's action. They treasured the sacred teachings transmitted by the great sutras with their whole heart.

Those who study Buddhism these days, however, recite glibly and seem to overvalue the writings of worldly scholars and Chinese classics, and request and cherish the poems of petty court officials. Furthermore, they have those writings written down on colorful paper and decorated with gorgeous silk. They can never have enough of this sort of literature, and consider them their utmost treasures. The treasures of students of Buddhism in the past and the treasures of students of Buddhism today are so different!

Although I am truly lacking in ability, I have cherished the old writings, and consider the sacred writings from the great sutras to be my greatest treasures. Still, these writings are too extensive, and the sea of sutras is so vast. I was afraid that fellow practitioners in the future might have to take unnecessary pains to weed through so many branches in order to gather the fruits that would truly nourish them.

So, in order to save students of the Dharma from such needless effort and trouble, I have selected here in one book a few hundred words from the writings that are the most essential and inspiring of faith in practice. The writings are spare, even deceptively simple, but their meanings are perfectly complete. If you consider this book your guide and pursue its truths to the end in order to attain the mysterious dharma, you will see a living Buddha sprouting out of each and every phrase. Therefore you should contemplate this book by all means.

Yet study these words and phrases though you may, it would be far better to attain that single word that is beyond all writings. It is a mysterious treasure outside all forms. I do not intend never to use it, but intend instead, from moment to moment, to wait for a special opportunity for it to manifest itself.

In summer, in the year of King Gap Ja
of the Era of Ga Jeong (1564)
In Cheong Heo Hermitage,

The Practitioner
Baek Hwa [one of Master So Sahn's epithets]

1

There is only one thing, from the very beginning, infinitely bright and mysterious by nature.

It was never born, and it never dies. It cannot be described or given a name.

Commentary

What is this "one thing"?

An eminent teacher wrote,

Even before the ancient Buddhas were born,
One thing was already perfectly complete.
Even Shakyamuni Buddha could not understand it.
How could he transmit it to Mahakashyapa?[1]

There is one "thing" that is never born, and never dies. For this reason it cannot be named in any way, or expressed, or depicted.

The Sixth Patriarch of Zen[2] once addressed the assembly thus: "I have something that has no name and no form. Do any of you see it?" Zen Master Shen-hui immediately replied, "It is the essence of all Buddhas, and also my buddha-nature." Due to this answer, Shen-hui cannot be considered a legitimate heir and descendant of the Sixth Patriarch.

Zen Master Nan-yueh came from Mount Seung Sahn to see the Sixth Patriarch, who asked, "What is it that comes here like this?" Nan-yueh was completely stuck, and could not answer anything. After eight years of practice, he finally attained en-lightenment and said, "If you even call this a 'thing,' it is not cor-rect." This answer is why Nan-yueh thus became the premier Dharma heir and successor of the Sixth Patriarch.

Gatha

> The sages of the three great teachings[3]
> Can be found in this phrase.
> Who dares express it must be careful—
> Your eyebrows may fall out!

2

The appearance of all Buddhas and Patriarchs in this world can be likened to waves arising suddenly on a windless ocean.

Commentary

The word *Buddha* refers to Shakyamuni Buddha, and *Patriarch* refers to the Venerable Mahakashyapa. Their coming into the world means that, out of great kindness and great compassion, they appeared in order to save all sentient beings from suffering.

In view of "the one thing," however, everyone's original nature is already complete, just as it is. Why have we come to depend on others, always wanting to dress up this simple matter with more powder and rouge? Therefore their coming into this world can be viewed in just the same way you would if waves were to somehow arise on a sea without wind. This is the reason why the *Maha Sunyata Sutra* says, "Words on a page are demon-karma, names and forms are demon-karma, and even the Buddha's own speech is demon-karma."[1]

All of this is just to say that when you correctly attain your original nature, both Buddha and Patriarchs are no longer of any use to you.

Gatha

Light fades away in heaven and earth,
When the sun and moon grow dark.

3

Yet, dharma has many depths of meaning, and people have different capacities to receive it. Therefore it is necessary to adopt different kinds of skillful means.

Commentary

Dharma[1] refers to the one thing, and people refers to all sentient beings. Dharma has two aspects: it never changes, and yet it also follows conditions, cause and effect. People also have two kinds of capacity: they always have the ability to awaken to themselves in an instant, while there is the constant need to refine themselves through gradual practices as well. Therefore it is necessary to adopt different kinds of skillful means employing words and speech. There is an old adage that goes, "According to official policy, even giving so much as a needle tip as a bribe is strictly prohibited. Yet in actual reality, horse-drawn carts laden up with bribes endlessly come and go."

Sentient beings' original nature is already complete, but they do not open their wisdom eye, and thus, of their own free will, fall into the cycle of rebirth (samsara).[2] Without the gleaming sword of Wisdom transcending worldly matters, who could cut through the heavy veil of ignorance?[3] Owing to the Buddha's great kindness and compassion, we are enabled to cross the ocean of suffering and arrive on the other side. Were we to sacrifice our life as many times as there are sands in the Ganges River, it would still be difficult to repay even the tiniest portion of this debt.

All of this demonstrates how much we should truly appreciate the blessings of the Buddha and the Patriarchs and redouble our efforts anew to attain our original nature.

Gatha

The king mounts the royal throne.
An old man in the countryside sings a song.

4

You may call it "mind," or "Buddha," or "sentient being."
Yet you should neither become attached to the names
nor make distinctions or understanding. The essence
of things is just-like-this. If even one thought appears,
that is already a mistake.

Commentary

Sutra teachings[1] rely on words such as these three names ("mind,"
"Buddha," "sentient being") to express the one thing. Zen meditation teaches that you must not become attached to any words or
speech.

Picking it up or putting it down. Creating or destroying. These
are the actions of a Free Person who is without any hindrance.

The selection above demonstrates how Buddhas and Patriarchs have freely used myriad expedient means to convey their
teachings.

Gatha

> It's like sweet rain falling after a long drought;
> Like encountering an old friend in a faraway,
>   foreign land.

5

The Zen meditation[1] tradition descends from the three situations where the Buddha transmitted his insight wordlessly from mind to mind.[2] The Sutra tradition derives from the occasions of the Buddha's spoken teachings, delivered throughout his life. Therefore it can be said that Zen is the Buddha's mind, while the sutras are the Buddha's words.

Commentary

Regarding the three situations of mind-to-mind transmission, the first occurred at the Pagoda of Many Children when the Buddha shared his seat with Mahakashyapa. The second was at the assembly at Mount Grdhrakuta (Vulture Peak) when the Buddha wordlessly held a flower aloft, but only Mahakashyapa smiled. The third was at the Buddha's funeral, when he projected his feet from inside the coffin. According to tradition, these three occasions mark Venerable Mahakashyapa's unique reception of the Zen lamp from the Buddha.

The tradition regarding the Buddha's words holds that he taught his disciples for forty-nine years. This tradition is sometimes viewed with regard to five kinds of teaching: the teachings that lead to good rebirth in human or celestial form; the Hinayana teaching;[3] the Mahayana teaching;[4] the teaching of

Sudden Enlightenment;[5] and the complete teaching on the Bodhisattva Way.[6] The Buddha's cousin and faithful attendant, the Venerable Ananda, unleashed this ocean of sutra teachings.[7]

Shakyamuni Buddha is the source of both the Zen meditation and the Sutra traditions, whereas the distinction in practice between the two traditions begins with Venerable Mahakashyapa and Venerable Ananda, respectively.

Zen meditation employs the wordless to reveal what is beyond words, whereas the sutras rely on words to express what is beyond words. So mind itself is the Zen teaching, and speech is the Sutra teaching. Dharma has but one taste, yet the difference between realizing it and merely understanding it—conceptually—is as vast as that between heaven and earth.

This section explains the distinction between the two paths of Zen meditation and sutra study.

Gatha

> Do not idle away your time wastefully,
> Or you soon find yourself
> stretched out upon the grass,
> reborn as a crawling thing or slithering snake.

6

If you become attached to words and speech, then even the Buddha's silently raising a flower or Mahakashyapa's wordless smile will be only another trace of the sutras. However, when you attain the truth within your own mind, even all the base chatter or elegant speech of the mundane world become nothing less than this same "special transmission outside the sutras."

Commentary

Dharma has no name, and so it cannot be grasped through words. It has no form, and so it cannot be understood through thinking. The instant you open your mouth to speak it, you have already departed from your original mind. When you lose this original mind, then even the story of the Buddha silently lifting a flower overhead and Mahakashyapa wordlessly smiling is, in the end, no better than dead speech to you.

If you attain the truth within your own mind, then even the senseless chitchat in the streets and markets are like the Dharma speech of a great teacher, and even a chirping bird or the wail of an animal express truth. For this very reason, when Zen Master Pao-chi heard the crying of bitter mourning, he awakened to his own mind and danced joyfully.[1] And Zen Master Pao-shou was suddenly enlightened to his true nature by the sight of a street fight![2]

This teaching expresses the depth and shallowness of the Zen meditation and scriptural traditions, respectively.

Gatha

A precious gem shining in the palm of your hand.
Playfully roll and rub it here and there.

7

I would like to say just one thing:
Cutting off all thinking, forgetting all
    conditions
While sitting here with nothing to do—
Yet spring comes, and grass grows all
    by itself.

Commentary

To cut off all thinking and let go of all conditions, all cause and effect—this is already attaining the truth within your own mind. You can then be called a true man of the Way who has nothing left to accomplish! How wonderful! Such a one is completely unfettered and from moment to moment does not make anything: When hungry, he eats; when tired, he sleeps. He wanders freely among the clear streams and blue mountains. He mingles easily and without hindrance in the busy ports and alehouses. The ebb and flow of time does not concern him, and yet spring comes and the green grass grows, as it always has.

    The essential point here is that whenever thinking arises, one should instead reflect inwardly on our own true mind's light.

Gatha

I wondered if there be
Such a person,
Anywhere.
But he's already here.

8

The Sutra teaching transmits only the dharma of One Mind, while Zen meditation transmits only the dharma of seeing one's true nature.

Commentary

Mind can be likened to a bright mirror's clear substance, while our true nature is like the mirror's reflective clarity. Our true nature is already pure and clear, as it is. The moment you attain enlightenment, you simply attain your original mind.

This emphasizes the importance of attaining moment-mind.

Gatha

> Seeing layer upon layer of mountains and
>   flowing streams
> Is itself my clear and bright original home.

Capping Word

Mind can be said to have two aspects: the fundamental mind, and the ignorant mind that is attached to forms and appearances. Our nature can also be described as having two aspects: a fundamental dharma nature, and a view where our nature stands opposed to forms and appearances. As a result of holding to any of these views, meditators as well as students of the sutras may remain in darkness. This happens whenever they become attached to names and cling to discriminating knowledge: Some argue that a shallow thing is deep, while others argue that the deep thing is shallow. This is a grave disease infecting both views and actions, so therefore I must comment so extensively here.

9

In all of the sutras expounded by the Buddha, he first draws distinctions between various kinds of Dharmas, and then only later explains the principle of emptiness. The Zen meditation tradition handed down from the Patriarchs teaches, however, that when all traces of thinking are cut off, the principle of emptiness appears clearly, of itself, as the very origin of mind.

Commentary

The Buddha is a teacher for all generations, so his teaching on the principle of emptiness is as complete and meticulous as is possible to communicate. On the other hand, Patriarchs awaken others to liberation directly, so their teachings are primarily focused on attaining sudden enlightenment. The term *traces* refers to the Patriarch's words, and *thinking* refers to the thinking of the student.

Gatha

> Contort your body as you may, and yet still
> You cannot bend your arm backward at the elbow.

10

The Buddha spoke like a bow, while the Patriarchs spoke like its string. He taught a no-hindrance Dharma that returns to the One Taste, sometimes called "substance." When even the traces of this "one taste" disappear, the one mind taught by the Patriarchs appears clearly. For this reason, it is said that the *hwa-du* of "the pine tree in the garden" cannot be found even in the sutras of the Dragon Palace under the sea.[1]

Commentary

"Speaking like a bow" has the sense of bending, while "speaking like its string" indicates straightforwardness and directness, or tautness. "The sutras of the Dragon Palace under the sea" refers to the vast collection of the eighty thousand sutras accumulated over the ages. A monk asked Zen Master Chao-chou, "What is the meaning of Bodhidharma's coming from the West?" Chao-chou replied, "The pine tree in the courtyard."[2] This is often called "a Zen teaching beyond any fixed forms."

Gatha

When fish swim, the water turns murky;
When birds fly, feathers flutter down.

11

Therefore students should understand the true teaching of the Buddha and distinguish clearly between the following two teachings: the fundamental ground of mind never changes, while at the same time the form of your mind conforms to causes and conditions. Students of the buddha-dharma should perceive how the two gates of sudden enlightenment and gradual practice are both the beginning and the end of their practice. Then they must put aside their sutras and meditate with total one-pointedness—only this will clearly reveal their mind. They will surely gain by this! Such is the way that you jump out of the burning house and save your life.[1]

Commentary

Teachings such as this do not necessarily apply to wise people of superior capacity, who are not bound by such limitations, but rather to practitioners of middling or inferior capacity, who cannot advance easily to such higher stages.

So, in sutra teachings one can distinguish between things that never change and things that change according to causes and conditions. Most people think that there is also a conceptual order between sudden enlightenment and gradual practice, suggesting that one follows after the other. In the Zen dharma, however, when you keep moment-mind, abiding at one point, things that never change and things that change according to causes and conditions, true nature and appearances, and substance and function are all realized as existing simultaneously. It is therefore extremely important that you abandon the view that things do or do not exist: everything is fundamentally the same True Suchness, as it is, and yet everything is clearly distinct.

For this reason, all the eminent teachers of the Zen school taught the dharma while abandoning attachment to words. They pointed directly to moment-mind, which is before thinking arises: "attain your true nature and become Buddha." This way is the true abandonment of the scriptural teaching.

Gatha

> On a clear and bright day,
> Clouds gather in deep valleys.
> In a remote and silent place,
> Radiant sunlight illuminates the clear sky.

12

It is extremely important that Zen practitioners should pursue live words, not dead words.

Commentary

If you attain enlightenment through live words, you will become a teacher equal to Buddha and the Patriarchs. If you attain through dead words, you cannot even save yourself.[1]

Therefore it is really only through "live words" that you can hope to be awakened to your own nature.

Gatha

> If you truly wish to see Zen Master Lin-chi,[2]
> You had better be a man of iron.

Capping Word

When looking into your Great Doubt (*hwa-du*, or *kong-an* [Jap.: *koan*]), there are two gates by which to enter: fiercely grabbing the key point of the *kong-an*, or merely grasping at the *kong-an's* conceptual meaning. Grabbing and holding fiercely the key point of the *kong-an* without letting go is to practice with "live words," which is a shortcut. It cuts off the path of mind and the path of speech, allowing nothing whatsoever to hold on to. Merely pursuing the conceptual meaning of your *kong-an* is practicing "complete" and "sudden enlightenment" teachings through attachment to dead words. Such study only opens wider the road to conceptual reasoning and the path of speech, since it is mainly concerned with thinking and conceptual understanding.

13

You should hold the *kong-an* with total determination, like a hen nesting on her brood, like a cat hunting a mouse, like a hungry man thinking of food, like a thirsty man thinking of water, and like a child longing for its mother. Only if you practice with this kind of mind are you sure to penetrate your Great Doubt.

Commentary

The Patriarchs left 1,700 *kong-ans*, such as, "A dog has no Buddha-nature,"[1] "the pine tree in the courtyard," "three pounds of flax,"[2] and "dry shit-stick."[3] A hen nests on her brood, always keeping them warm. When a cat chases a mouse, its mind and eyes never wander from the object of its hunt, no matter what. A starving man has but one object: food; a man with throat parched from thirst conceives of but one goal: get water. A child who has been left alone for a long time by its mother only longs to see her again.

All of these focused efforts come only from the deepest mind, and are not artificial. It is a kind of intense sincerity. Without such a deeply straightforward striving mind, it is impossible to attain enlightenment.

14

Three things are essential in Zen meditation. The first is Great Faith. The second is Great Courage. The third is Great Doubt. If any one of these is missing, it becomes like a tripod cauldron that is missing one leg—it is of no use at all.

Commentary

The Buddha said, "Faith is the ground for attaining Buddhahood." The Venerable Yung-chia said, "Those who would attain the Way must firmly establish their will."[1] Venerable Meng-shan said, "To one who practices Zen meditation, the gravest disease is a *hwa-du* without Great Doubt."[2] And he also said, "If you strongly keep Great Doubt, always and everywhere, you will surely attain great enlightenment."

15

You should constantly raise your *hwa-du* in the midst of whatever you do in daily life, ceaselessly investigating, "Why did Zen Master Chao-chou say that a dog has no buddha-nature?" Eventually the path of reasoning and the path of conceptual meaning will be cut off. Though you eat, there is no taste, and you will feel hemmed in on all sides. This is the point where you throw away both body and life. This is the point where you can become a buddha or a Patriarch and all that.

Commentary

A monk asked Zen Master Chao-chou, "The Buddha said that all things have Buddha-nature. Then does a dog have Buddha-nature?" Chao-chou replied, "No." This one word is the front gate of the Zen School. It is a tool to utterly destroy all wrong views and false understanding. It is also the true original face of all the buddhas and the bone of all Patriarchs. Only after having penetrated this gate can you become a buddha or a Patriarch. An ancient eminence expressed the value of Zen Master Chao-chou's "No!" *kong-an* in this verse:

The fearsome sword of Chao-chou
Glitters like an ice needle.
Whoever dares to ask what it means
Their body will be sliced in two.

16

When you raise your *hwa-du,* your *kong-an* or Great Doubt, never attempt to figure out some correct answer, nor pursue it with thought. And do not just wait around until you become awakened. If you arrive at the place where thought cannot enter, your mind will have nowhere to go. It will be for you like an old rat that has entered the trap made of an ox horn: there is no way for retreat, and seemingly no way forward, either. It would be complete delusion to calculate this and that, to wander here and there following the karma of life and death, and to run about in fear and confusion. These days, people do not know that this is a sickness, and keep falling in and out of this sickness over and over and over again.

Commentary

There are ten sicknesses to avoid in *hwa-du* practice: trying to figure out the *kong-an* using discriminative thought; seizing on the master's wordless teaching gestures, such as raising his eyebrows or winking; allowing yourself to get caught by words and speech; searching for proofs or evidence in the *kong-an;* miming the shout or sudden expression of some master as if it were your own thing; abandoning everything by falling into emptiness; attempting to distinguish between conditions of existence or nonexistence; thinking in terms of absolute nothingness; knowing things in terms of logical reasoning; and impatiently expecting awakening.

You must completely avoid these ten sicknesses! Instead, firmly holding the Great Doubt inspired by the *kong-an*, and keeping your mind clear, pour all of your energy into the question "What is this?"

17

This matter of *hwa-du* practice can be likened to a mosquito biting an iron bull. The mosquito does not try to figure out, "Do I do it this way, or that?" Its needlelike mouth pressed firmly on the impenetrable, it risks body and life, in one moment penetrating through with its whole being.

Commentary

This teaching recalls the point made earlier about the "live word." It is restated here in order to protect those who look deeply into the live word from regressing in their practice. An eminent teacher said, "Those who practice Zen must penetrate thoroughly the gate of the Patriarchs: in other words, to attain profound enlightenment, simply cut off the mind-road!"

18

Correct meditation practice is much like tuning the strings of an old lute: find the right chord between too tight and too loose, and beautiful music can appear. But overexertion makes you prone to all kinds of attachment, while negligent, inattentive practice leads only to deeper ignorance. It is best to practice Zen with a calm and clear mind—constantly attentive and not-moving.

Commentary

Any lute player can tell you that the strings of a harp must be properly tuned—neither too tight nor too loose—in order to make beautiful music. Practicing meditation follows the same principle. Impetuous practice makes you overstimulated and distempered, while slackened practice leaves you dulled and vague, and leads you right into the cave of demons. When your practice is neither too "slow" nor too "fast," you will find the mysteriously subtle balance in it.

19

There will eventually be a point in your practice when you do not know you are walking even as you walk, and do not know your are sitting even as you sit. In this situation, Mara's legions of the 84,000 demons guarding the gates of the six sense faculties will rise up and attack you the moment any kind of mind appears.[1]

But when any kind of mind does not appear, what harm can they do?

Commentary

Mara is the name of a ghost or demon that actually relishes the suffering of birth and death. Eighty-four thousand demons mean the eighty-four kinds of suffering that beset sentient beings. Mara originally has no self-nature, but appears only when practitioners lose their fundamentally pure and clear moment-mind. Sentient beings are attached to whatever appears, so they yield to the circumstances of Mara. True students of the Way are not deluded by appearances, so they confront Mara: they are not taken in by delusive circumstances. This is why it is said, "The steeper the path is, the more demons you will find."

When delusions appear in your mind, demons seem to appear before you, too. A practitioner once hacked at his own leg during meditation when he saw a mourner, and another encountered a pig and grabbed his own nose![2] If your mind does not move, however, all the diabolical skills of Mara employed against your mind will come to nothing, like someone trying to cut water with a sword or to blow away a ray of sunshine. An ancient adage says, "A crack in the wall will let the wind blow in; a crack in the mind lets demons sneak in."

20

When any kind of mind appears, this is the entrance of the Demon King. The mind that does not appear is the Five-Skandhas Demon. The mind that both appears and does not appear is the Mara of Passions. Yet in true Dharma, these so-called demons do not, in fact, exist.

Commentary

"No-mind" is the buddha-way, while all conceptual discrimination is the way of demons. In any event, the existence of demons is just the workings of a dream. Why worry and agonize over it so much?

21

Were you to attain but a little progress in meditation practice, at the moment of death you would not be dragged under by the force of negative karma, even if you have not attained enlightenment in this lifetime.

Commentary

Karma is merely the darkness created by our defilements. Zen meditation is a bright wisdom. It is only natural that darkness is not something that can remain in the presence of light.

22

Zen practitioners should always reflect on themselves, and consider deeply these questions: Are you aware of the Four Kinds of Debt? Do you know that your body, a temporary composite of the four elements, is deteriorating moment by moment? Do you know that your life hangs tenuously on a single moment's breath? Do you constantly reflect on the diminishing good merit that has enabled you to meet the teachings of the Buddha and the Patriarchs during this rebirth? Do you know how rare and precious it is to meet the supreme and holy Dharma? Do you remain within the temple precincts, and abide by the precepts of a true practitioner? Or do you waste away your time chatting about senseless things with the people around you? Do you constantly provoke disagreements? Is your *hwa-du* clearly seen, no matter what the activities of the day? Do you continue to pursue your *hwa-du* even while talking with others? Is it the same when you are seeing, listening, or perceiving? Is your practice enough to seize and defeat the Buddha and the Patriarchs? Can you faithfully transmit the Buddha's wisdom in this life by any means necessary? Do you think of hell's suffering when you sit or lie down in comfort? Are you confident that you will escape samsara with the body given you in this life? Is your mind unmoving even when the eight winds[1] are blowing?

These are essential questions that every student of the Way must constantly reflect on in the midst of everyday life. For as one ancient worthy said, "If I cannot save this body even in this life, in what lifetime could I ever possibly save it?"

Commentary

The Four Kinds of Debt are the indebtedness to parents, to country, to teacher, and to the donors who have materially supported our practice. The four elements that constitute our filthy body are earth, air, fire, and water. The humid *ch'i* (energy) of water comes from the mixture of a drop of your father's sperm with a drop of your mother's blood. The solid *ch'i* of your bones and flesh comes from the earth element. Your blood does not rot into a lifeless clot or thin out due to the hot *ch'i* of fire. Finally, your nostrils appeared before anything else in order to enable breathing, which depends on the movement of the *ch'i* of wind.

The view that considers this body as "filthy" is derived from the Venerable Ananda's saying, "Base and full of impurity is sensual desire, for the enjoyment of sensual desire entails the mixing together of filthy, stinking substances."

Our body is constantly deteriorating, from one moment to the next, and since time never stops, it leaves behind the mark of wrinkles on your face and gray hair on your head. There is an old saying: "Today's appearance is already unlike yesterday's

appearance. Tomorrow's will surely be unlike today's. . . ." Indeed, the body is completely ephemeral. The demon of impermanence takes luscious pleasure in killing: this condition alone
should terrify us out of our wits every moment of the day! In-
halation and exhalation are the *ch'i*s of wind and fire, respectively. So in a way our life is utterly dependent on these fuels
mutually feeding each other. The Eight Winds are eight types of
circumstances that either suit you or go against you. Regarding
hell's sufferings, mentioned above, a day in hell equals sixty *kalpas*
(aeons) in this world.[2] The sufferings of hell are beyond any description: plunged into molten metal and searing flames, dragged
through mountains of swords and forests of jagged spears. This
is what truly awaits you!

Being reborn as a human is far rarer and more difficult than
finding a needle that has fallen to the bottom of the deepest sea. I
warn you of these things only out of great pity for your condition!

Capping Word

Mere intelligence, however great, cannot in any way dilute or
restrain the force of one's self-made karma. That is the essential
message of the teachings above. Dry wisdom—a wisdom of con-
cepts, learned things—cannot save you from endless rebirth in
the ocean of suffering. Rather, from moment to moment you
should look inward, carefully reflecting on what you see. Only
then can you be sure of not deceiving yourself. It is like drinking a glass of water: Only you can know for yourself whether it
is hot or cold.

23

There are those who study only words and speech, who may seem to be enlightened when they open their mouths to speak. In reality, however, when faced with everyday situations, they become so flustered that they do not know what to do. This shows the difference between the nature of words and the nature of actions.

Commentary

This expands on the main point of the preceding section: the danger of self-deception. Our words must accord with our deeds; speech and actions must be one. Only in this way can we distinguish truth from falsehood.

24

If you do not wish to be touched by life and death, you must firmly hold the "one thought" and break through in a flash. Only there can you be truly freed from life and death.

Commentary

When a thickly painted lacquer bucket is smashed, it emits a great sound: *Bang!* You must smash to pieces the heavy lacquer bucket of your own delusion in order to cut off life and death. At some point in their search for Buddhahood, all buddhas have attained this action, and nothing more.

25

And yet even though you have broken through the appearance of even a single thought, you must still find a keen-eyed master to check whether you have attained a correct insight.

Commentary

It is extremely difficult to attain enlightenment. So you should be very careful, even humble about any sense of attainment. The Dharma is like the vast sea: the farther you dive, the deeper it is. Only the truly foolish would allow themselves to be satisfied with some small attainment. Even experiencing some sort of breakthrough, you must still meet a keen-eyed master to have your insight verified: failing to do this, even the rarefied taste of *manda* (refined exotic Indian milk) may well turn into venom.

26

An ancient worthy once said, "I do not concern myself so much with your behavior. My sole concern is that you attain correct insight."

Commentary

A long time ago, replying to a question posed by his teacher, Zen Master Wei-shan, Venerable Yang-shan said, "The forty volumes of the *Nirvana Sutra* are all pure demon speech." Such was Venerable Yang-shan's keen eye. When Yang-shan proceeded to ask his teacher about the importance of behavior, or deportment, in his practice, Master Wei-shan replied, "I do not concern myself so much with your behavior. My sole concern is that you attain correct insight."[1]

27

My hope is that all practitioners of the Way completely believe in their true self. You should neither lack confidence nor give rise to pride.

Commentary

Mind is fundamentally equal and the same, and thus there is no real distinction between "ordinary people" and "sages." Nevertheless there are, in reality, those who wander in darkness and those who have been awakened to their true nature, thus distinguishing "ordinary people" from "sages." Following the instruction of a teacher, a practitioner may attain, in an instant, his true self, thereby realizing that he is ultimately no different from the Buddha. Hence it is said, "Originally, there is nothing," which means simply that one must not underestimate oneself, and lack confidence. This is the teaching of "sudden enlightenment."

Even after attaining some realization, however, one must always strive to cut off lingering mind-habits so that one can be fully transformed from an "ordinary person" into a "sage." This is the teaching of "gradual cultivation," emphasizing that we must "polish the clear mirror from moment to moment." This is why pride can be such a hindrance. Lacking faith in one's own nature is the sickness of those attached to scriptural authority, whereas pride is the disease of those who practice only Zen meditation.

People who are attached to sutras and a scriptural teaching of words can lack faith in the living, mysterious experience of meditation that leads to a sudden insight. They are usually too caught up in the expedient means of words and speech, attached to the stubborn habit of distinguishing between "true" and "not true." Believing only what is written in holy texts they are conceptually mesmerized by the treasures of others, instead of digging inside to discover the priceless gems of their own, lying deep within. As a result, such people retrogress spiritually of their own accord.

Zen students, on the other hand, often lack proper faith in the sutras, and so disregard the scriptural teachings on gradualist cultivation and eliminating harmful mind-habits. They are not ashamed even when these defilements and karmic habits arise in their mind. Foolishly proud of their so-called "dharma" long before their practice can be said to have truly matured, their speech can be seen only as pure arrogance.

Therefore, those who practice correctly must not lack confidence in their true nature, nor should they give in to pride.

Capping Word

In the beginner's mind—the basic wish for enlightenment—is contained the seed within the fruit: one need only believe in one's primary point, our true nature. For this reason practitioners need not lack confidence. However much one believes in this seed, the fruit that is bodhisattvahood develops through fifty-five stages.[1] There is a gradual cultivation of any seed into a fruit. For this reason practitioners must not overestimate themselves, giving in to feelings of pride.

28

Practicing the Way with a deluded mind merely adds to one's ignorance.

Commentary

How can you say that you practice correctly if you have not yet attained even a little insight? Enlightenment and gradual culti-vation feed each other like oil and fire, guide each other like eyes and feet.

29

The point of practicing is simply to cut off worldly thoughts. The enlightenment experience of all saints and sages is nothing other than this.

Commentary

When the sickness is cured, medicine is no longer necessary. You merely return to what you originally are.

30

It is really not necessary to try to discard the mind of a sentient being. And searching for something like "correct" dharma is also a big mistake. Simply strive to keep your true self from becoming defiled: that is all.

Commentary

"Seeking" and "discarding" are both mistakes.

31

To practice cutting off all defilements is to practice a dualistic way, whereas just keeping the mind where no defilements arise is called "nirvana" (liberation).[1]

Commentary

"Cutting off" anything is itself the trap of dualistic thinking, since it assumes opposites such as subject and object. But when nothing whatsoever arises in the mind, how can even "subject" or "object" appear?

32

To empty your mind, simply reflect deeply right into it. Then you can truly have faith that, in reality, the appearing and disappearing of even one thought is itself an illusion: There is, in fact, no "thing" that ever actually appears.

Commentary

These words point out how to have correct insight into original nature.

33

If you just look deeply into things, you see that killing, stealing, unchaste conduct, and lying all arise from this One Mind.[1] And when the ground from which these defilements arise is seen to be empty and perfect stillness, what defilement could ever arise?

Commentary

This teaching explains the relationship between our original nature and appearances.

Capping Word

Another sutra puts it this way: "When even a single thought does not arise, ignorance is already cut off." It goes on to say, "The moment a thought arises in your mind, awaken right then and there!"

34

If you know that the arising thought is itself unreal delusion, you are already free. What need is there for employing skillful means? Freed from any delusion, you are already enlightened, so there is no need for gradual progress.

Commentary

We can say that our mind is like a magician. Then this body is like a magically conjured castle, the world merely a set of fantastically conjured clothing, and names and forms are just magically conjured food. Any mind that arises is illusion, and even raising a single thought is illusion. Then how much more so are the illusions created by speaking of "right" and "wrong," and "true" or "false!"

These beginningless illusions are all ignorance, and yet they appear out of our fundamentally awakened mind-ground. They are like flowers seen in an empty sky, possessing no real substance whatsoever. When all such illusions are realized as being not truly there, it can be said that one has reached a stage of stability, or "not-moving mind." The one who calls for a doctor in his or her dream, believing they are sick, is freed from that "sickness" the moment they wake up. The same is true for one who attains the realization that everything is pure illusion.

35

Sentient beings abide in complete stillness, with nothing moving in the least: nothing appears or disappears. It is sometimes called "the birthless." Yet they make the delusion of "life" and "death" and "Nirvana/salvation," and believe that they are real, like seeing flowers appearing and disappearing in the sky.

Commentary

Our True Nature never appears, so there is no life or death, and no Nirvana or salvation. You could say that it is like vast empty sky with nothing moving in it: If you think of life and death, you are like someone who might see flowers suddenly appear in the empty sky; and to think Nirvana or salvation is like someone who suddenly sees flowers disappear from the sky. But there is nothing there! What seems to appear has actually never appeared, and what seems to disappear has actually never disappeared. Therefore it is pointless even to argue either of these two views. This is why the *Su-yi Ching Sutra* teaches, "The Buddha did not appear in this world to save sentient beings. Rather, the Buddha appeared in order to liberate this world from the mistaken view that there is life and death, and Nirvana or salvation."

36

We can sometimes say, "Bodhisattvas save sentient beings by leading them into Nirvana." And yet, in reality, there are no "sentient beings" who attain any kind of "Nirvana."

Commentary

From thought-moment to thought-moment, bodhisattvas are supremely devoted to saving sentient beings. But in truth, saving all sentient beings merely consists of attaining, in one moment, the realization that the substance of each thought is essentially empty. That is all. When all thinking is seen to be empty and completely not-moving, you attain that there are, in fact, no "sentient beings" in need of "saving." These words explain the real nature of faith and enlightenment in the buddha-dharma.

37

It is entirely possible to attain a sudden enlightenment, whereas in actuality, mind-habits cannot be eliminated just as instantly.

Commentary

Manjushri Bodhisattva attained and taught the realization of the nature of universal substance.[1] Samantabhadra Bodhisattva emphasized the more gradual, incrementalist way of gaining insight into dependent origination, causes and effects.[2] One way teaches like a flash of lightning, while the other teaches the inching progress of a little child.

38

Practicing Zen meditation while remaining immersed in sexual concerns is like cooking sand for a meal. Practicing Zen meditation while yet not avoiding killing any living thing is like a person who plugs their own ears and then shouts something important to himself. Practicing Zen meditation with a mind that would steal is like trying to fill a leaky bowl. And a liar who practices Zen meditation is a person who would try to use feces for incense. Even for the one who has much wisdom, such failings can only lead you to the way of demons.

Commentary

This illuminates the most basic guidelines for our practice. It encompasses the traditional threefold practice (precepts, meditation, wisdom)[1] through which we can cut off the karmic outflows (sensual craving, desire for becoming, attachment to false views, ignorance). In the Hinayana tradition, precepts are used to receive the Dharma and also help us to live by it. In a manner of speaking, these are the "outer nature of the precepts," and keeping them is an end in itself. Mahayana students use precepts to seek their mind, cutting off "mind" at its root.

Therefore, in the Hinayana, precepts protect the Dharma by
teaching us not to violate it with the actions of our body, while
the Mahayana emphasizes keeping "mind precepts" so that we
do not stray from the Dharma through the arising of our thinking
mind. Lust blots out our pure nature. Killing living beings cuts
off our innately compassionate mind. Taking things not given
cuts off our good fortune, merit, and virtue. Lying cuts off the
truth of things as they are. For though you have already attained
some insight and may even possess the six supernatural powers,
you will fall onto the path of demons and be forever denied ac-
cess to these teachings of perfect enlightenment unless you ab-
stain from killing, stealing, lustful attachment, and deception.[2]

These four precepts are the foundation for all of the precepts.
They are explained here at such great length to prevent you from
violating them even in thought. Not following after the thinking-
mind is what is meant by "precepts" (*sila*). Not giving rise to thinking, but keeping a mind before thinking arises is what is known as
"meditation" (*samadhi*). And not being guided into action by foolish thought is what is known as "wisdom" (*prajna*).

Put another way, precepts capture the thief—our deluded
mind, our defiled mind; meditation ties up the thief; and wisdom kills the thief. Only a strong, uncracked bowl made from
the precepts can contain the pure, clear water of meditation, reflecting wisdom like the moon on its surface.

This threefold practice is the foundation for all the countless
dharmas. It has been explained here specifically to prevent all of
the karmic outflows. Had the Buddha, who enunciated this threefold practice, been reckless in his teaching? Or perhaps even Bodhidharma, who reiterated it, should be accused of telling lies?

39

People lacking in virtue do not rely on the Buddha's precepts, nor do they maintain vigilance over the three kinds of karma (karma of thought, speech, and action). Such people lead a lazy and dissolute life, looking down on others and provoking quarrels.

Commentary

Once you break the precepts—even in your mind—then every imaginable misdeed will appear as well.

Capping Word

Those who practice the Dharma should always keep in mind that, in an instant, legions of karmic demons can spread like a flash fire. Their intent is to distort and taint these teachings on how to find a correct way and correct life. It is especially true during this period of the decline of the Dharma.[1]

40

If you do not abide by the precepts, in your next rebirth you will not even be able to receive the body of
a mangy fox. How, then, can you even imagine attaining the fruit of pure wisdom by living like this?

Commentary

You should abide by the precepts as if, by doing so, you were
serving the Buddha himself. Then it is as if the Buddha were constantly with you. Take as models the monk who endured being
tied and bound with living grasses by thieves,[1] and the monk
who refused to report the goose that swallowed a priceless gem,
preferring instead to absorb the blame and scorn of others who
believed that he had absconded with the jewel, rather than see
the goose be killed to have the gem removed.[2]

41

To get out of the cycle of life and death, it is absolutely essential that you first cut off your desires and lusting.

Commentary

Attachment is the root cause of our endless transmigration through birth and death. Is it not enough to see that the lust that our parents kindled in each other was the condition that produced our own bodies? The Buddha said about this, "You will never shake off the dust of defilement and delusion if you do not cut off the lusting mind." He also taught, "Once you let yourself get tangled up in sensual desires, you are soon dragged to the gate of error." "Burning with desire" and "burning passion" are terms we use often in everyday life; they show that constant desire and lusting are to our mind as flame is to dry wood.

42

Pure and clear wisdom that functions with no hindrance arises from correct meditation.

Commentary

The power of meditation (*samadhi*)[1] can turn even a middling person into a sage. Through *samadhi*, people have also gained the power to die while sitting up straight or even while standing. As an eminent teacher once said, "If you seek the Way of the holy ones, there is really no path apart from meditation."

43

When mind is plunged into meditation (*samadhi*), one perceives clearly the appearing and disappearing of things in the world.

Commentary

> Tiny dust motes float down
> Through sunlight gleaming in a window.
> The glassy surface of pure, still water
> Reflects back the world, just as it is.

44

If while encountering myriad situations your mind does not give rise to thinking, this is what we mean by "unborn." The "unborn" nature is "before thinking," and before thinking is itself "Nirvana," or salvation.

Commentary

The threefold practice of precepts (*sila*), meditation (*samadhi*), and wisdom (*prajna*) is a holistic unity, and any one of them cannot be practiced separately from the others. To practice any one of them entails practicing all three.

45

Some people may be under the impression that we practice dharma in order to attain Nirvana.

But this is a mistake. Mind is originally calm and perfectly clear, just as it is. Attaining this realization is true "Nirvana," or salvation. That is why it is taught, "All dharmas are originally marked by Nirvana."

Commentary

Your eyes cannot see your own eyes. So it would be false to say that you can see your own eyes. This explains why, when challenged to explain the principle of nonduality, Manjushri Bodhisattva resorted to conceptual thinking, but the layman Vimalakirti answered the same question by remaining silent.[1]

46

If a poor man comes begging from you, give him what he needs according to your means. Have great love and great compassion, considering him as if he were part of your own body. This is true charity (*dana*), true sharing, true giving.[1]

Commentary

"I" and "you," "self" and "other" are not two, but one body. We all came into the world empty-handed, and will leave empty-handed. That is our life.

47

Though someone may injure you in some way, you must keep a settled, not-moving mind. Do not give in to anger or resentment. When even a single angry thought appears in your mind, countless obstacles are born.

Commentary

Defilements of the mind are numberless. Anger is the most severe. The *Nirvana Sutra* teaches, "You should be able to keep a not-moving mind in any condition and any situation, whether someone slashes you with a dagger or someone massages you with fine water and precious, scented ointment." The momentary flashing of anger is like lightning bursting from an empty cloud.

48

If you have no patience, the limitless compassionate functioning of the six paramitas cannot be attained.[1]

Commentary

There are an infinite number of different ways to practice, but compassion and patience are the basis for all of them. An eminent teacher said, "If mind itself can be seen to be no more real than the dreaming action of a lifeless puppet, then even the worst insults heaped upon you are no more real than hair sprouting on a tortoise."

49

Just maintaining the original, true mind is the supreme practice.

Commentary

The mind that consciously thinks "I am practicing" or "I will practice" is not truly practicing, but rather deluding itself. This is why the old Zen master used to answer every question put to him, "Never delude yourself! Never delude yourself!"[1]

Lazy people always put things off to the future, thinking they will practice "then." This is nothing less than giving up on yourself.

50

As to the use of mantras: It may be relatively easy to control karma made in the present life, so you can correct it through your own effort. However, the karma accumulated over many previous lives is very difficult to erase. For this work you must rely on the mystic power of repeating a mantra.[1]

Commentary

According to the *Surangama Sutra*, one day the Venerable Ananda was approached by a lowest-caste woman, who used a mantra on him to lure him into her room. The bodhisattva Manjushri intervened, employing another, more powerful mantra to release Venerable Ananda from her charms. The woman eventually shaved her head, and upon hearing just one teaching from the Buddha, attained enlightenment.

It is not false to claim that this lowest-caste woman indeed attained the fruit of the Dharma. So we can see from this that it is very difficult indeed to avoid the grasp of delusions without using the transcendent power of mantras.

51

True prayer requires *devotion* and *surrender*: You must be faithfully devoted to your true nature, and then you can make ignorance surrender to it.

Commentary

Body, speech, and mind return to perfect purity and stillness: This is how a Buddha appears in the world!

52

Merely chanting with the lips is nothing more than recitation of the Buddha's name. Chanting with a one-pointed mind is true chanting. Just mouthing the words without mindfulness, absorbed in habitual thinking, will do no real good for your practice.

Commentary

The six-worded dharma practice of chanting "NAMU AMITA BUL" can be a shortcut road for cutting through the cycle of trans-migration.[1] But when you chant this, you must remain focused one-pointedly on the realm of the Buddha, reciting the Buddha's name clearly and without clinging to any passing thoughts. When your mindfulness accords with the sound produced by your lips, completely cutting off all thinking, this can truly be called "chanting."

Capping Word

The Fifth Patriarch[2] once said, "It is better to keep your true, original mind than to contemplate the Buddhas of the ten direc-tions."[3] The Six Patriarch said, "If you only contemplate other Buddhas, you will never break free from life and death. You should keep your buddha-mind as it is in order to arrive on the other shore." And he taught further, "Buddha originates in your own nature. There is no need to seek outside yourself." He also said, "Ignorant people chant in the hope of being born in the Pure Land, or Land of Utmost Bliss, but true practitioners only focus instead on clearing their own mind." Also, "The Buddha does not save sentient beings. Rather, sentient beings save themselves the instant they awaken to their true mind." These eminent teachers pointed directly to our original mind, without depending on skillful means: there is no other teaching than this.

And yet, however direct and effective such teaching may be, we must also be able to say that paradise and Amita Buddha with his forty-eight vows really do exist.[4] Therefore it is taught that one who recites Amita Buddha's name even ten times will attain rebirth in a lotus flower, thus escaping the cycle of birth and death. This teaching has been given by all the Buddhas in the three divisions of time;[5] all bodhisattvas of the ten directions vow to attain such a rebirth, too. The stories of those who have been reborn this way—either in the past or in the present—have been faithfully handed down to us. So it is hoped that no practitioners hold to mistaken views, and simply practice hard.

Amita is a Sanskrit word meaning "infinite life" and "infinite light," and is used as a name for the Buddha of the ten directions and the three divisions of time. As a younger practitioner, he was called Venerable Dharmakara ("Store of the Dharma"). Making the forty-eight vows before Lokesvararaja Buddha, he proclaimed, "When I attain to buddhahood, should any of the numberless devas or humans residing in the ten directions—even down to the tiniest insects—chant my name but ten times, I will cause their rebirth in my heavenly realm. I hereby vow never to enter fully into Nirvana until this vow is accomplished."

Ancient sages in other times pronounced similar practices: "The sound of chanting even a single word weakens even demonic forces, and erases one's name from the lists of the dead in Hell. Instead, one is reborn as a lotus flower in a pond of purest gold." The Repentance Dharma teachings expand on this, saying, "We can use our own innate power for spiritual practice, and we can use the spiritual power of others. Progress through reliance on the former is slower, while the latter is fast. Imagine two men who wish to cross a vast sea: One man plants trees, raises them through hard work, cuts them down when they are grown, and makes a boat. Then he attempts his journey. This is what it is like to rely solely on your own power. But another man simply borrows someone else's boat and crosses the sea directly. Anyone can see that this is a faster method. It can be likened to relying on the power of the Buddha in our spiritual practice."

This sutra also says, "A child who is threatened with fire or rising waters cries out desperately, and his parents rush to save him. In the same way, when a man chants the name of the Buddha, even in the hour of his death, the Buddha will greet him with mysterious powers. The Buddha's great love and great compassion are greater even than the love of a parent for their child, because sentient beings' torment in the ocean of life and death is even more excruciating than anything inflicted by fires or floods."

Of course, there are people who may hear teachings like this and say, "Nonsense! Your own mind is already the Pure Land.[6] There is no such thing as being reborn in some such place!" Or "This is low-class teaching! Your own true nature is Amita Buddha, not different. There is not some 'other' Amita Buddha who meets you!"

Such words might have some truth to them, but they are not the whole view. The reality of our condition is different from just those views. Amita Buddha is perfect, having neither desire nor anger. But are we free from desire or anger? The Buddha is known to be able to change a raging hell into a world of lotus flowers just as effortlessly as you might turn your hand over. And yet do we who live in hourly fear of tumbling headlong into hell due to the unstoppable momentum of our karma ever change this hell into lotus flowers? The Buddha perceives infinite billions of galaxies as your or my eye might perceive an object right in front of our nose. And yet we cannot see the things that are happening outside the thin walls of this very room, much less perceive the infinite billions of galaxies in every direction!

In the same way, though at the most fundamental level our nature is the very nature of Amita Buddha, our actions are those of sentient beings. The former and the latter, the ideal and the reality, are as far apart as heaven and earth. Master Kuei-feng was clearly aware of this when he said, "Even one who attains sudden enlightenment in the end must do continuous, gradual practice."[7] How right he is!

Now let us turn again to the one who claims that he is already the same as Amita Buddha and ask him, How is it that Shakyamuni Buddha was manifested at the urging of this universe? And how is it that an Amita Buddha could appear as such a spontaneous manifestation?

You can only truly understand if you reflect deeply within yourself. When you find yourself suddenly being pulled through death's door, and there is no recourse back, are you unshakably confident that you can find the freedom taught by the Buddhas even in that moment? If not, then you should fully examine your foolish pride to see whether it would not be better for you to discard that right now, lest it trick you into the hellish torments of a lower rebirth!

Great Patriarchs of the dharma though they were, even such as Asvaghosha[8] and Nagarjuna[9] must have felt this, for they always emphasized the crucial importance of striving toward a good rebirth in our next life. Then who are we to disregard so easily the matter of our next rebirth? The Buddha himself declared the importance of our diligently striving: "The Pure Land of the Western Paradise is far, far from here. You must pass 100,000 lands, and even 8,000 more regions, in order to reach it." Thus he freely employed words about space and distance to give an almost visual sense, for the sake of leading those of dull perceptions, to prod them on. But in other places he said with equal sincerity, "The Pure Land of the Western Paradise is not a faraway place. Why? Because the very mind of sentient beings is the place of Amita Buddha." This teaching reveals his free use of expedient means for leading those of quicker faculties.

So we can see from all of this that the teachings can freely use seemingly different expedient means and expressions to point to the same universal substance. Only the words themselves have a different appearance and meaning, yet the point they communicate is the same. For one whose insight is in accord with his actions, it is possible to see through what is said to be "near" or "far." This is why our tradition can embrace both ways of practice: calling out to Amita Buddha, like Hui-yuan,[10] and looking directly into true nature, like Jui-yen.[11]

53

When you hear sutras being chanted—either by your own voice or by other people—you are cultivating affinity for the teachings and practice. It is a Way that leads to a joyful mind and great spiritual merit. This body is no more stable than a bubble: it will soon disappear. But any efforts made for the sake of truth will never die.

Commentary

These words point to truly wise study: It is like one who ingests a priceless diamond; this is something greater than just receiving and holding the seven other most precious gems.[1] Zen Master Yung-ming said, "Even if you hear the Dharma teachings, though you may not necessarily have complete faith in their meaning, nevertheless a seed has been planted that will eventually result in your becoming a buddha. And then even if you study these teachings yet still fail to attain their true meaning, you have nevertheless made enough merit that you cannot fail to be reborn as a human or *deva* (heavenly spirit)."[2]

54

When studying Buddhist sutras, if you do not reflect deeply on your own mind at the same time, you could study the entire 84,000-volume canon of the Buddha's words and still it would not do you any good whatsoever.

Commentary

The previous chapter described the inner nature of wise study of the sutras; this teaching tells how one may do the same study unwisely. Just mouthing or reading words without interior reflection on mind makes your actions no different from those of a bird chirping on a spring day, or an insect buzzing through an autumn night. Kuei-feng taught, "Just reading the sutras and chasing after the literal meaning of the words themselves, from its very origin, is study that cannot lead you to an awakening. Interpreting texts and analyzing the meaning of words merely produces heaps of desire, anger, and ignorant, mistaken views."[1]

55

Using clever words and eloquent speech to show off to others your knowledge of the Dharma, especially if you have not had any awakening, is like colorfully painting a stinking outhouse to make it look like a temple.

Commentary

This teaching points right at the goings-on in these days of decline of the true Dharma, with foolish people spouting off so glibly about their so-called "teachings." Practicing the Dharma originally meant simply looking deeply into one's True Nature. But many people do this to show off something that is not really theirs. What on earth has gotten into their heads?

56

Someone who is devoted to studying the Dharma—
especially those who leave home to become monks and
nuns—who study things like novels and other material
that has no relation to the Way is like someone who
would cut mud with a priceless jeweled sword. In the
end, the mud is base and useless material, but what is
most distressing of all, the sword is only dulled thereby.

Commentary

> Children of a good family,
> Playing freely outside
> Without a care in the world,
> Reenter the home blazing with fire.[1]

57

Who could ever think that becoming a monk is a trivial thing? Such a decision is not for someone seeking a leisurely, comfortable life. It is not for someone who wishes to have fine clothing or good food, nor is it for someone who desires fame or riches. The homeless life of monks and nuns is possible for one who strives to cut off life and death by eliminating all defilements of the mind. This path should be chosen by those who wish to ensure correct transmission of the Buddha's wisdom, transcending the three worlds (conditions of desire, form, and no-form) and ferrying sentient beings across the ocean of suffering to the other side.[1]

Commentary

The home-leaver is indeed peerless! Peerless!

58

The Buddha taught, "Absolutely everything is totally aflame, burning with the fire of impermanence." And at another time he said, "Sentient beings are always engulfed in raging flames of suffering." He warned us further, "Passions and delusion are like a vicious enemy who is always looking for an opportunity to kill you." Anyone who studies the Dharma should heed these words! We must practice with the terror and urgency of one who suddenly realizes that his head has caught fire.

Commentary

This impermanent body is born, grows old, becomes sick, and eventually dies. The universe and everything in it appears, is stable for some time, disintegrates, and eventually returns to emptiness. Likewise, mental conditions appear, remain for some period of time, change, and then disappear.

You must see clearly that suffering seems so endless only because the flames of impermanence rage everywhere. The one who wishes to perceive what is true in the midst of impermanence must not waste time, for this is truly a life lived in vain.

59

Craving recognition, social approval, or the other empty labels of this world is like the mind of a person who would deliberately put a gash in their own body. Chasing after material gain just dumps more fuel on your own karmic flames.

Commentary

Someone once wrote the following verses to describe the mind that craves the labels and names of this world:

> Like a wild goose that flies to the end of the sky,
> Leaving only footprints behind for a time on
>   the sand,
> When a person dies, and goes to another world,
> Only their name is left behind with the family.

There are also verses on the relentless chase after material gain:

> Nectar gathered from a thousand flowers
> Produces such golden, delicious honey.
> But who is this one who hasn't lifted a finger
> And yet smacks his lips with the taste?

We have seen above how the person who craves the empty names of this world is like a person who would purposely wound their own body for no reason. Such a thing is utterly useless to do, like trying to carve a piece of ice into a timeless masterpiece of art. Dressing up fashionably, applying the latest expensive perfumes and makeup in order to attract others, is just an everyday example of "dumping more fuel on your karmic fire."

60

A patch-robed monk who seeks fame or fortune cannot even be compared to some country rustic dressed in shabby clothes.

Commentary

It is well known that the Buddha virtually spat on the royal throne he was supposed to inherit, preferring instead a hard life of spiritual austerities in the snow-covered Himalayas. This kind of steely attitude is the iron rule of our Buddhist tradition. And though a thousand buddhas may appear tomorrow, this attitude toward finding the Way will never change. Yet in this period of the decline of the Dharma, herds of sheeplike practitioners posing in borrowed tiger skins will lead younger practitioners with crass impunity. You can see them, the ones who are always jumping on the bandwagon of popular opinion about what the Dharma "is" or "should be." Such people as this end up only becoming attached to the little power that accrues to their positions, accustomed to the flattery of this kind of life. Unbelievable! What could ever change minds like these?

Annotation

Those whose minds become tainted with the stench of wealth or fame always cling to the powerful. They become overly involved in worldly affairs and are considered to be ludicrous even by the nonreligious. Especially when someone like this is an ordained monk or nun, we call them a sheep in borrowed clothing. But their every action reveals them for what they are!

61

The Buddha once lamented, "Look at this! Thieves wear robes to represent my teaching, and yet they only make all kinds of intense karma by selling me for their own personal profit!"

Commentary

In this age of the Dharma's decline, there are many epithets given to errant monks. Among the most frequently used are "bat-monk," "deaf-mute goat-monk," "bald layman," "hell scum," and "thief in a monk's robe."

Capping Word

Whoever denies the teaching of cause and effect (karma) and the connection between our mental deeds and the positive or negative merit they produce is called "someone who sells the Buddha for a living." Their bodies and mouths boil with flame, as they ceaselessly produce feelings of "like" and "dislike." What a shame!

The Chinese character for *bat* means "bird/rat," and yet a bat is neither one of these two. So "bat-monk" is often used to refer to an ordained monastic who is neither monk nor layman. A "deaf-mute goat-monk" is what we call a monk who does not teach the dharma. Some monks, though they dress and appear like monks, continue to keep the mind and attitude of a layman: this is a "bald layman." A monk who is completely trapped by the weight of all the negative karma he has made is "hell scum." There is also the "thief in a monk's robe" who just makes a nice living off of selling the Buddha and his teachings. These various names have been used differently for each kind of monk, but at bottom what they all really mean is "thief in a monk's robe."

62

Oh, students of Buddhism! The food you receive every day comes from the blood, sweat, and bitter tears of hardworking farmers. And your clothes come from the hard labor of the weavers. How will you ever wipe away the heavy karma incurred through receiving these things for free if you are not making constant efforts to open your True Eye?

Commentary

The Record of the Transmission of the Lamp says, "A practitioner in ages past did not make a strong effort to find his True Nature, despite receiving offerings. After his death he was reborn as a mushroom to repay the faithful for their support."[1]

63

It has been said, "Would you like to really know how a being entering rebirth in this world takes on fur and hide and horns, and inhabits the lower animal realm? For this is surely the future course of one who receives temple offerings but does not practice diligently." And yet despite the fact that teaching like this is repeated again and again, some practitioners eat even when they are not hungry and acquire more clothing even though there is no need for it. How pitiful are these! What could possibly be going on in their minds? Such people should stop and consider for a moment how the pleasure they enjoy today is definitely measured back to them as suffering in their next rebirth.

Commentary

The *Maha Prajnaparamita Shastra*[1] relates the story of a monk who was reborn as a cow because he wasted merely five grains of hulled millet. As a cow, he repaid part of the karmic debt through years of hard labor, and only finished the debt with his hide and meat and bones after death. The law of cause and effect (karma) merely functions as an echo rebounds from sound: Wasting the offerings of Buddhist faithful creates a debt that must be repaid, no matter what.

64

And so an eminent teacher said, "It would be far better to wrap your body in white-hot iron than to put on the clothing offered by people out of faith. It would be better to drink a cup of molten metal than accept food from people offering through faith. And it would do you more good jumping into a furnace of molten iron than staying in the house donated by offering through faith."

Commentary

The *Brahamajala Sutra* says, "Vow to receive neither food nor things offered by the faithful when you have broken the precepts. A bodhisattva who cannot live by such a vow as this commits a minor transgression."[1]

65

For this reason it has been taught, "Practitioners should receive their food as if it were poison. They should accept offerings as if receiving arrows shot into their body." Practitioners of the Dharma should also be extremely wary of kind treatment and flattering words.

Commentary

"Receiving their food as if it were poison" means that you should always be on guard against losing your eye for the Way. And "accept offerings as if receiving arrows shot into their body" simply warns you not to lose the fruit of this Dharma.

66

A person practicing the Way can be likened to a whetstone. When Buddhist faithful come to increase their store of spiritual merit by making offerings to the monks, it is knives being sharpened on the whetstone: the knives become sharp, but the stone is worn down by this. And yet despite this, there are still some practitioners who always worry that people may not come to sharpen their knives on this whetstone.

What a pity!

Commentary

Such a practitioner as this has only one wish in his life: to have hearty meals and warm clothes provided for him.

67

An ancient saying goes, "The agony of the Three Evil Paths is not true agony. A suffering that far surpasses this is that suffered by one who has worn monks' robes yet still loses his human body in the next rebirth."[1]

Commentary

An ancient worthy said, "If you cannot attain awakening in this life, you will not be able to digest even a single drop of water." This is the meaning of the expression "one who has worn monks' robes yet still loses his human body." Oh, students of the Buddha! Let such words fill you with regret in order to inspire your efforts!

68

Having a body is so distressing! Filthy matter is constantly dripping and oozing from its nine holes, and hundreds of thousands of polyps and boils are bound together by a very thin layer of skin. Imagine a fragile leather sack filled to the brim with feces and bloody pus. It is constantly stinking and filthy: what is there to covet here? And what is most ironic is that, despite the care and worry of a hundred years' effort on your part, all the kindness and work you have given to protect this thing will be rudely repaid when the body ceases, in a single breath.

Commentary

All of the karmas mentioned in the above sections only appear because of having this body. If you looked deeply into this bodily condition of ours for just a moment, you would scream out loud. If nothing else, this alone should truly shock us into practicing! The body is the root of all desires and attachments, so if you practice hard and attain that it is an empty illusion, then all desires and attachments will disappear by themselves. But attachment to our bodies is what draws us into all manner of vice and regret, suffering and anxiety. So I only go to such length and description as this simply to open practitioners' eyes.

Capping Word

This physical body of ours is sometimes referred to as the "four-fold enemy." This is simply because it is a temporary material conglomeration of the four elements (earth, air, fire, and water), and the four elements have no master, no "I." It is also called the "four snakes" since it will repay your years of kindness to it with ingratitude. You are angered by others, or belittle them, only because you have not yet realized the empty, unreal nature of your own body. And when others behave similarly toward you, it is because they also have not realized this point. When people grow angry at each other or look down on each other, it is no different than two ghosts fighting over a corpse!

This is because our corpselike body is really just a fragile heap of bubbles no more substantial than a dream. It is a pile of sufferings and a sack of feces. It is constantly rotting and always filled with filth. The seven holes in the upper part of the body continually ooze tears, mucus, and puslike things, while the lower orifices constantly ooze urine and feces. Countless are the efforts we must spend, every day of our lives, just to keep the body clean enough that it does not offend when we spend time with others. This is why it has always been said that beneficial spirits will immediately abandon the man or woman who is impure.

The *Sutra on Cause and Effect* addresses this when it says, "Those who hold a sutra with unclean hands, or spit in front of a Buddha statue, will be born as an outhouse worm in their next life."[1] And according to the *Sutra on the Perfection of Wisdom in Seven Hundred Verses*, "Even when defecating or urinating, one should be as indifferent as a tree or rock, not speaking or making any sound. And of course you should not scribble things on the walls or leave the bathroom space unclean with your spit."[2] The sutra goes on to teach, "One who has not washed his or her hands completely after using the toilet should not just as mindlessly return to their meditation cushion, or go directly to pray in a Buddha hall."

69

Repent immediately when you commit a misdeed, feeling shame when you realize that you have done something wrong: this is the character of a great person. When you correct your failings in this way, constantly renewing yourself by reflecting on your mind, bad karma will disappear and you will always live in accordance with your true nature.

Commentary

True repentance means first to regret the misdeed you have committed and then to vow not to repeat it in the future. Being ashamed of yourself means to objectively reflect on yourself inside and to manifest some change on the outside. In any event, mind is originally empty and completely still, so there is actually no place where bad karma can remain.

70

Those who would truly practice this dharma must keep a not-moving mind, taking simplicity and truthfulness as their standard. Dressed in humble, even rough clothing and carrying a hollowed-out gourd for freely drinking in mountain streams, they will not be hindered wherever they go.

Commentary

The Buddha said, "The mind should be maintained like a taut string." And he also said, "The not-moving mind is itself a holy temple." Completely unattached to your feelings, condition, and situation, you can come and go anywhere with no hindrance.

71

Mediocre people run hither and thither, constantly chasing circumstances as if they were objects. Students of this dharma seek their mind. However, the highest dharma means letting go of both dharma *and* objects.

Commentary

Those who chase after circumstances are like thirsty deer that run after a shimmering mirage, mistakenly believing that the mirage is actually water. Those who try to grasp at their mind are like monkeys who try to grasp at the reflection of the moon on the water. Grasping at circumstances and grasping at mind are different, but in a sense they are both diseases. This teaching describes the nature of ordinary people and of those practicing according to the Two Vehicles.

Gatha

> In heaven and earth, there is neither the sun
> Nor the moon of the Chin Dynasty.
> In rivers and mountains,
> Where are either the ruler or the ruled of the
> Han Dynasty?

72

Mara, Lord of Demons, can catch a *sravaka* even when he is deeply engaged in meditation in the forest.[1] However, heretics and Mara cannot detect a bodhisattva, even though he wanders freely through all quarters of this mundane world.

Commentary

A *sravaka* (voice-hearer) believes that true practice means meditating in stillness and quietude. Because of even this much attachment to something, his mind moves, and whenever mind moves, demons can see it. On the contrary, a bodhisattva is one awakened to the truth that True Nature is fundamentally empty and still, just as it is. So a bodhisattva leaves no traces of any kind. Therefore the heretics and Mara cannot see anything about the bodhisattva. This teaching clarifies the differences between the path of the Two Vehicles and the path of the bodhisattva.[2]

Gatha

> Flower petals drift freely onto the path, following the wind.
> But a house appears gloomy when cloaked in falling rain.

73

In the hour of your death, simply perceive: the five *skandhas* are intrinsically empty;[1] the four elements composing this body have no "I"; our True Nature has no mark, no shape, or form, and does not come or go, appear or disappear; when your body was born, True Nature is not born, and when you die, True Nature does not die; perfectly quiescent and still, mind and objects are not two things.

If you can attain to this realization, in an instant you are no longer bound or deceived by cause and effect in the three worlds [of desire, form, and formlessness]. Such a one can truly be called "free," one who has really transcended the world and all that. Though the Buddha appears, this person is not excited; when even hell appears, he is not fearful in the least. Attaining no-mind, you and the whole universe are never separate. This is a very important thing to realize!

Every day of your life you unknowingly sow seeds of karma, and the fruit appears at death. Whoever does not open their eyes and look closely at this is indeed foolish in the extreme!

Commentary

People suddenly become interested in getting close to the Buddha through practice after growing old and feeling the approach of death![2]

Gatha

> This very moment is the time to make an effort,
>> because
> A hundred years pass by in the twinkling of an eye!

74

If in the hour of your death you make even the slightest distinction between the enlightened and unenlightened, holy or unholy people, you will be inexorably pulled into your next rebirth through the womb of a donkey or a horse, or stuffed into an iron furnace raging in hell, or become an ant or a mosquito.

Commentary

Zen Master Pai-yun once said, "And even if you do not make the slightest distinction between the enlightened and the unenlightened, you may still fall into your next rebirth through the womb of a donkey or a horse."[1] If any two opposite views pass through your mind, even as remote possibilities, you still run the risk of entering one of the various lower rebirths!

Gatha

> A great fire rages all around.
> Yet still, the gem-encrusted sword glints.

Capping Word

These two verses in particular express the great Patriarchal Gate through which people are urged to attain liberation simply by realizing their not-knowing mind, the mind before any thinking arises. Such teachings are an expedient means for closing off the usual gates through which many people strive to travel, namely such practices as the gate of chanting to Amita Buddha just for the purpose of obtaining rebirth in some paradise.

At the same time, we can say that the two gates do not contradict each other. People's capacities differ, and their purposes and aims in life are different. So therefore many expedient means are available.

I merely hope that those who would practice this dharma do their very best according to their particular condition and situation. Please do not risk the possibility that doubts or regrets may arise in the last moments of your life!

75

How can someone who has not unshakably attained his mind's original nature possibly penetrate the gate of Truth, which somehow appears to be so distant? You often hear people claim that Zen meditation is just about attaining an emptiness that completely cuts off everything. Others claim that enlightenment is about an emptiness of inexpressibility. And still others have the opinion that "all things do not exist."

Entertaining ideas such as these is the worst kind of blindness, the worst of diseases. Among those who practice or speak so glibly of Zen nowadays, how many can we honestly say are free of such sicknesses?

Commentary

The highest gate of liberation actually has no ground for you to step on. Zen Master Yun-men put it this way: "Two kinds of sicknesses prevent you from seeing your True Nature. But even after you have penetrated your True Nature, another two kinds of sicknesses will hinder you."[1] Therefore it is of utmost importance that you penetrate your nature from moment to moment.

Gatha

> If you do not cross the meadow thickly covered
>   in weeds,
> You will never reach the village dusted with
>   falling blossoms.

76

Great teachers may also have many sicknesses. Those whose ears and eyes are afflicted will express their practice by focusing energy intensely in their eyes, or by tilting their ears and nodding their head knowingly. For those who have a sickness in their mouth and tongue, Zen is about spouting nonsensical phrases or giving a sudden shout of "HO!" even though they are not awakened to its meaning themselves.[1] Those whose Zen sickness is expressed in the limbs may step forward, then backward, or wordlessly draw a line in the air.

Those who have a Zen sickness in their hearts or innards will claim their truths, affecting an air of mysteriousness, or by arrogantly setting themselves above "the ignorant masses" and spouting all sorts of declarations about them. In the end, all such attitudes and gestures just make more and more sickness.

Commentary

One who kills his parents may repent to the Buddha. But those who defame this wisdom teaching have no way to repent.

Gatha

> Even grasping at shadows in the empty air
> Is ridiculous enough.
> How much more so is someone who claims to have
> Special meanings outside of things as they are?

77

Masters who are truly awakened will show the Dharma clearly and simply. But yet they reveal it like a wooden doll that sings, and what they express is as ungraspable as snowflakes falling on a searing furnace, or like a flash of lightning: None of their expression has a form by which you can know it, hold it. Students have no way to possess it from them. This is what an eminent teacher meant when he said, "I do not respect my teacher's virtue so much as I am forever indebted to him for not cheating me with conceptual or intellectual explanations of the Dharma."[1]

Commentary

>Don't say a thing! Do not say a thing!
>It might end up being put into writing!

Gatha

>An arrow piercing a reflection of the moon on
> the river
>Really comes from the bow of one who hunts eagles?

78

Students should first distinguish in detail the branches of the various Zen schools. Once upon a time, at a single shout from Zen Master Ma-tsu,[1] Pai-chang[2] turned deaf and Huang-po's tongue hung down from his mouth.[3] This one shout was the very same news that the Buddha communicated in raising a flower, and also the original face that Bodhidharma revealed upon first coming to China. All of this became the foundation of the Lin-Chi School.

Commentary

We must fear most a person who thinks he knows the Dharma. I will hit him the moment he opens his mouth to speak it.

Gatha

> A wooden staff without crook or joint
> Is quietly given to a traveler journeying by night.

Capping Word

At a single shout of Zen Master Ma-tsu, Pai-chang attained great substance, and Huang-po attained great function. Great substance is perfectly complete and conforms to any condition or situation. Great function means to just do it, moment to moment, effortlessly responding to conditions. The foregoing stories are all set down in great detail in *The Record of the Transmission of the Lamp*.

79

There are five schools, or "houses," in the transmission of Patriarchal Zen: the Lin-Chi School, the Ts'ao-Tung School, the Yun-Men School, the Wei-Yang School, and the Fa-Yen School.

Lin-Chi School

This school traces direct descent from the Great Master Hui-neng, the Sixth Patriarch of Zen, and the thirty-third dharma successor from our great teacher, Shakyamuni Buddha. The dharma successors of Hui-neng are as follows: Nan-yueh Huai-jang, Ma-tsu Tao-i, Pai-chang Huai-hai, Huang-po Shi-yun, Lin-chi I-hsuan, Hsing-hua Ts'ung-chiang, Nan-yuan Hui-yung, Feng-hsueh Yen-chao, Shou-shan Sheng-nien, Fen-yang Shan-cha, Tz'u-ming Ch'u-yuan, Yang-ch'i Fang-hui, Pai-yun Shou-tuan, Wu-tsu Fa-yen, Yuan-wu K'o-ch'in, and Ching-shan Tsung-kao.[1]

80

Ts'ao-Tung School

This is a lateral branch of transmission separated from the school of the Sixth Patriarch. Its dharma successors are as follows: Ch'ing-yuan Hsing-ssu, Shih-t'ou Hsi-ch'ien, Yüeh-shan Wei-yen, Yun-yen T'an-sheng, Tung-shan Liang-chieh, Ts'ao-shan Tan-chang, and Yun-chu Tao-ying.[1]

81

Yun-Men School

This is a lateral branch originating out of Master Ma-tsu. His dharma successors are as follows: T'ien-huang Tao-wu, Lung-t'an Ch'ung-hsin, Te-shan Hsuan-chien, Hsueh-feng I-ts'un, Yun-men Wen-yen, Hsueh-tou Tsung-hsien, and Tien-i I-huai.

82

Wei-Yang School

This is a lateral branch of transmission originating with Master Pai-chang. His dharma successors are as follows: Wei-shan Ling-yu, Yang-shan Hui-chi, Hsiang-yen Chih-hsien, Nan-t'a Kuang-yung, P'a-ch'o Hye-ch'ong, Huo-shan Ching-t'ung, and Wu-chao Wen-hsi.

83

Fa-Yen School

This is a lateral branch of transmission originating with Master Hsueh-feng. His dharma successors are as follows: Hsuan-sha Shih-pei, Chi-tsang Kuei-ch'en, Fa-yen Wen-i, T'ien-T'ai Te-shao, Yung-ming Yen-shou, Lung-chi Shao-hsiu, and Nan-tai Shou-an.

84

Lin-chi's shout and Te-shan's staff wordlessly reveal the truth of our fundamental birthlessness, confirming it from top to bottom. These are two masters who had thoroughly attained great substance and great function, moving freely in all places. As a no-hindrance expedient means, they manifested themselves in bodily form, and shouldered the burden of passing on this tradition to us in these days. In so doing, they preserved for our eyes and ears the sacred wisdom realm of Samanta-bhadra and Manjushri.

And yet throughout all of this effort, in truth these two forces manifesting as great masters were, in form and essence, no more substantial than ghosts.

Commentary

> Watch out when handling a sharp blade,
> Or you may get hurt!

Gatha

> Glittering ice needles? or are they real gems
>   bouncing on the water?
> In a sky clear of any clouds, the moon drifts away.

85

The superior person beholds the Buddhas and Patriarchs as if he were spying an enemy. He knows that if, in his search for truth, he becomes attached to the Buddha, he is hindered by the Buddha. If he is attached to the Patriarchs, the Patriarchs hinder him. Whenever you seek something outside your own mind, everything is suffering. It would be far better to just have nothing to do!

Commentary

The first verse—"the superior person beholds the Buddhas and Patriarchs as if he were spying an enemy"—ties in with a teaching given in chapter 2 of this text: "The appearance of all Buddhas and Patriarchs in this world can be likened to waves arising suddenly on a windless ocean." The verse "Whenever you seek something outside your own mind, everything is suffering" corresponds to a phrase from chapter 4: "The essence of things is just-like-this." The verse that says, "It would be far better to just have nothing to do" caps the teaching from chapter 4: "If even one thought appears, that is already a mistake."

If you could just attain what all these teachings are pointing to, you would cut off the meaningless speech of everyone in the world, even while seated in meditation. Through your practice and attainment, the wheel of life and death will stop by itself.

Even a great struggle to end a war or establish peace and harmony in society are not acts greater than Tan-hsia burning a wooden statue of the Buddha,[1] or Master Yun-men declaring that he would have fed the newborn Buddha to a hungry dog,[2] or the old lady's refusal to meet the Buddha.[3] All of these actions were no-hindrance expedient means for cutting off untruth and revealing truth. In the end, what is there really left to do that is as important as all that?

Gatha

> I always miss March
> On the south side of the river,
> Where partridges sing and the fragrance of
>   blooming flowers
> Hangs in the air.

86

The sacred radiance of our original nature
    never darkens.
It has shined forth since beginningless time.
Do you wish to enter the gate that leads
    to this?
Simply do not give rise to conceptual
    thinking.

Commentary

When we say, "The sacred radiance of our original nature never darkens," it is in direct reference to the very first line of this text: "There is only one thing, from the very beginning, infinitely bright and mysterious by nature." The verse "It has shined forth since beginningless time" also completes the phrase "It was never born, and it never dies." And the teaching "Simply do not give rise to conceptual thinking" completes the phrase from chapter 4, "You should neither become attached to the names nor make distinctions or understanding." Having a gate implies clearly that there is a way through that both ordinary people and experienced practitioners can enter. For exactly this reason Venerable Shenhui once said that "true knowledge" is entered "through the mysterious gate of not-knowing," quoting Lao-tze.

So the entire teaching of this text began with the statement that "It cannot be described, or given a name" and ends, here, with the exhortation, "Simply do not give rise to conceptual thinking." This cuts off all entangling views in a single phrase: simply don't know.

Our whole text begins and ends by pointing to the nature of knowing, of what is true knowledge. And in between we have cited all kinds of virtues and practices. Intellectual, conceptual, word-based knowledge and knowing are a potent threat to realizing the Buddha's dharma. So this is why we cannot fail to return to this point of "What is true knowledge?" here at the conclusion. And for this same reason, Master Shen-hui, though he practiced with the Sixth Patriarch before the latter established a thriving community on Chogye Mountain, cannot be regarded as a legitimate holder of the Chogye lineage that succeeds to this day. It was precisely his reliance on intellectual views and mere conceptual understanding of the Dharma that cut him off from the Patriarchal lineage.

Gatha

> All of this effort, spent
> Setting out the teachings in such detail.
> And yet wouldn't this, too,
> Cause our founder Bodhidharma to laugh out loud?
> But is there any other choice?
>
> HO!!!
>
> The bright moon now shining down;
> Mountains and rivers are calm and still.
> Laughing at this whole enterprise, even at myself,
> Also startles heaven and earth!
>
> Ha ha ha ha ha!!

Epilogue

BY A STUDENT OF
ZEN MASTER SO SAHN

The foregoing text was written by the Venerable Do-Eun [Zen Master So Sahn], an eminent Master of the Chogye Order of Korean Buddhism.

Alas! Buddhism in Korea has steadily deteriorated over the last two hundred years, and the band of monks who lead the Zen School and the other band of monks who emphasize scriptural study have staked out their differing opinions as to the direction of our study. Those emphasizing scripture study over meditation developed a taste for lesser things, and these sorts of monks are as plentiful as sand. They do not know that there is a path wherein human beings can be enlightened from *within*, without reliance on the five scriptural traditions. After all, our teaching points directly to the original mind, doesn't it?

Meanwhile, those who emphasize exclusively the practice of Zen meditation above all else only believe in their original purity. So they may often look down upon the role of gradualist practices. They often disregard the importance of setting one's mind on attaining the most perfect knowledge after attaining a sudden enlightenment; and people focused exclusively on Zen meditation practice may overlook the power of doing the myriad practices through which the moment-to-moment function of that enlightenment is honed and perfected.

For reasons such as this, the respective roles of Zen meditation and scriptural study are often confused, in the same way as it becomes difficult to separate gold from sand. This is what the *Complete Enlightenment Sutra* points out: "Some say that, since man is born with buddha-nature, and is already complete, there is neither 'illusion' nor 'enlightenment.' For this reason, they ignore the existence of cause and effect. This is a wrong view. On the other hand, some say that instantaneously attaining our original nature is an illusion because ignorance can only be overcome through gradual practice. For this reason, they lose sight of their true and changeless nature. This is also a mistaken view."

Oh, how perilous it can all be!

Why is it so difficult to correctly transmit this Way?

In fact our tradition had always been on the verge of falling, like a single strand of hair that holds ten thousand pounds suspended in space, when our old Master sat down to write this book. He used any spare time he could find, while feeding cows for ten years on Western Mountain (So Sahn), to assemble this. He pored over fifty volumes of sutras and their related commentaries, and jotted down only the clearest and most essential words that he found in them. Then he taught these things directly to us, his disciples, showing us the love of a shepherd for his flock: feeding his charges with loving-kindness, he taught restraint to those who were in excess and goaded those who were lazy or fell behind. This was all done for the single purpose of leading them right to the gate of Great Enlightenment.

However, his students were so dull that his high and difficult dharma talks still caused them trouble. Thereupon our old Master had pity on them, and added these explanatory Commentaries to each phrase and put it in a certain order. As a result, all the phrases came to be threaded on a single string, and blood began circulating, bringing the teaching alive for them.

This text contains the essence of the eighty thousand sutras and the bone of the Five Schools of Zen. Every word reveals truth, and every phrase accords with the overall teaching direction that he intended. Study of this text will moderate those who are troubled with excess, and those who are hindered will break through. This text is indeed a mirror of Zen meditation as well as the sutras, a very effective medicine for true knowledge and its function, for sudden enlightenment and gradual practice.

It must be known that our old Master always spoke of the teaching matters contained herein with utmost discretion. As if walking on the edge of a sharp knife, he actually feared that even a single word or half of a phrase might end up in any such written record as this. Therefore to circulate this widely or to take pride in his ability were the last things he would have wanted. Among his disciples, Zen Master Baek Un Bo Won copied it, and Master Byeok Chon Ui Cheon edited it. Thereafter disciples such as the Great Master Jeong Won, the Great Master Dae Sang, and Cheong Ha Boep Yung gave a deep bow and highly praised this text as an unparalleled work. Along with six or seven other monks, they begged enough money to have it engraved on woodblocks for further circulation. It was distributed widely in order to repay our old Master in some humble way for his great compassion in teaching and awakening us.

The deep truth of the Buddha and the subtle dharma of the Patriarchs are like a vast ocean: If you wanted to search for the precious gem contained in the mouth of a great dragon living at the bottom of the sea, at what point of the vast ocean surface would you enter? And what would guide your search? Unless you have the means to move around under the sea just as freely as walking on land, you could not but lament as you are left sitting on the shore.

Therefore our Master's great achievement in selecting the essence of our teachings, and his compassion in awakening us, are as high as a mountain and as deep as the sea. Even were you to grind your bones a thousand times, or sacrifice your life ten thousand times, you would never be able to repay even the smallest bit of this great kindness he has shown us.

Simply do not become astonished or doubtful when you hear and see this teaching. If you read it with respect and make it your treasure, this text will become a bright light to guide you, not only through this life but in life after life after life.

> These words are written down in Spring, in the year of King Gimyo of the Manryeok era (1579).

> Bikkhu Yu Jeong, in the lineage of the Chogye Order of Korean Buddhism, bowing in reverence to these essential teachings transmitted from our Teacher by word of mouth, humbly in this epilogue offers these closing words.

Notes

Chapter 1

This is a symbolic way that some masters have employed to represent—outside of any words—the perfectly complete "nature of mind," our "nature," "true self," "essence." Even though we call it these things, and also here "one thing," you should not associate your nature with any material quality or form or attribute. "True suchness" might be the best we can do in words. The Great Master Seng-ts'an (?–606), the Third Patriarch of Zen in China, wrote in *Xin-Xin-Ming* (*Verses on Faith-Mind*), "It is like vast emptiness. There is nothing lacking, and nothing is in excess."

So we artificially name it "mind" or "nature" or "truth" or "Tao," but actually no name fits it at all. There is no way to describe its true form, to draw or say it either. It fills infinite space, yet has no inside or outside. It covers infinite time, while supposing no iota of "then" or "now," and even then has no beginning or end. You cannot argue that it has "large" or "small," "many"

or "few," "high" or "low," "true" or "false," "sacred" or "profane,"
"holy" or "unholy."

For want of any nearer expression, let us just temporarily
refer to it as a perfect sphere. Anyway, you cannot adequately
express its true meaning, no matter how hard you may try. Hence
if you were to dare to teach it, we would say, "Opening your mouth
is already a big mistake." Another eminent teacher said, "The true
way does not depend on understanding or non-understanding."
It is sometimes said that one must "get enlightened" and "become
a buddha." But if you already possess this "enlightened nature,"
from your very origin, then it is redundant to aspire to "become
a buddha"! Hence the famous phrase, quoted by Master So Sahn
here, "Even Shakyamuni Buddha did not understand it./How
could he transmit it to Mahakashyapa?"

1. Mahakashyapa: One of Shakyamuni Buddha's ten leading
disciples, he entered the Order at a relatively advanced age.
Though Brahmin by birth, and despite having advanced to a high
priestly status in Hindu society, his late ordination put him under
the rank of others who had ordained with the Buddha before him.
The Zen tradition posits Mahakashyapa as the First Patriarch of
Zen: According to hallowed tradition, when the Buddha lifted an
udambara flower on Vulture Peak, only Mahakashyapa smiled in
tacit recognition, causing the Buddha to pronounce that only
Mahakashyapa had received his "True Dharma."

2. Sixth Patriarch: The Chinese monk Hui-Neng (638–713)
is often referred to as the Sixth Patriarch. Shen-hui (670–762;
dates approximate) and Nan-yueh Huai-jang (677–744) were
two of his foremost disciples.

3. Sages of the Three Teachings: Shakyamuni Buddha of Buddhism, Lao-Tze of Taoism, and Confucius of Confucianism.

Chapter 2

1. Karma: Activity of mind caused by thoughts, words, and deeds. Sometimes translated as "mind-habit." The Buddha originally taught that one must avoid impure or "bad" karma, and strive instead for pure or "good" karma. In the end, as the student's practice matures, he showed how one must transcend both "good" and "bad," pure and impure. One must not be attached to feelings of sin or bliss, or even to the teachings propounding a holy way.

Chapter 3

1. Dharma: In a general sense, "law" or principle, rule or "natural way," reality and suchness. In Buddhist contexts, it refers to the Buddha's teachings, his doctrines, discourses, and henceforth the teachings of all Buddhist teachers.

2. Samsara: Literally, the wheel of suffering, or the cycle of transmigration through endless birth and death. The accumulated habit-force of thoughts and actions committed over countless rebirths, samsara is cut through in an instant of self-awakening, the Buddha taught.

3. Ignorance: In Sino-Korean, literally "mind darkness." According to the "Discourse on the Awakening of Faith in the Mahayana Way," there are two dimensions to ignorance: one is "fundamental ignorance," which is any arising of thought that obscures insight into the nature of reality as it is, or dharma; the other kind of ignorance might be termed "derivative ignorance,"

which is the minute, crude, delusional thoughts subsequently springing out of that fundamental obscuration.

Chapter 4

1. Sutra: The oral teachings of the Buddha that were later committed to writing and gathered as scriptures.

Chapter 5

1. Zen [Sanskrit: *dhyana*; Chinese: *ch'an*; Kor.: *soen*; Jap./English: *zen*]: Literally, "meditation."

2. Three occasions of mind-to-mind transmission: Three situations emphasized by the Zen school wherein the Buddha wordlessly transmitted his mind-dharma to Mahakashyapa: The Buddha was teaching on one occasion at the Pagoda of Many Children, before an assembly of many hundreds of monks. Mahakashyapa entered the assembly late. Since he was a relative newcomer to the Buddhist sangha, or "Order," it is said that his lateness may have been displeasing to some of the elder monks. Yet instead of automatically taking a seat among the younger ordinands, he proceeded directly to the front, to where the Buddha sat. As he approached, the Buddha moved over slightly on his reed mat, granting a revered place, which Mahakashyapa instantly assumed. With this wordless gesture, admitting such a young monk as Mahakashyapa to his own seat, the Buddha revealed for the assembly the universal equality of all buddhanature, or "substance." Another occasion was the gathering at Vulture Peak, where in lieu of a spoken teaching the Buddha silently raised an udambara flower aloft before a vast assembly: only Mahakashyapa, seated in the far back, smiled in tacit recognition of truth as-it-is. And then, at the site of the Buddha's cremation, Mahakashyapa circumambulated the funeral pyre three

times, and bowed thrice. At this, the Buddha's feet suddenly protruded out of the funeral mound, revealing to a startled community that, though the Buddha's physical body may have expired, buddha-nature has no life or death.

3. Hinayana teaching: A somewhat pejorative term coined by the later self-proclaimed "Mahayana" (Great Vehicle) school to refer to the earliest teachings of the Buddha, emphasizing personal salvation through meditative and ethical practices. The term *Hinayana* (Lesser Vehicle) is not used by any school or tradition to represent itself; rather, it was strictly created from the point of view of the later traditions that sprang up in northern India after the Buddha's death. According to the Mahayana view, the Buddha initially taught a "man is god" way—considered a lower, simplistic path to enlightenment—so that primarily monastic-oriented practitioners could cut off their thinking and defilements as a means of reaching the peace and extinction of Nirvana. The Hinayana is also referred to by Mahayana practitioners, of whom Master So Sahn is a representative, as the Two Vehicles because, in the Mahayana view, it presents essentially two paths: one is to perceive the Four Noble Truths and become a voice-hearer, a "holy one" or *sravaka*; the other is to gain insight into the Twelve Links in the Chain of Dependent Origination, thereby attaining the state of a solitary awakened one, or *pratyeka-buddha*. Both paths, however noble, are deemed to be self-oriented—even selfish, according to some Mahayana commentators—because their concern is less with the effort to save all beings than with the striving for individual salvation. Because he represents a tradition whose pejorative intent is implicit, and because it is important to any full understanding of his view, throughout Master So Sahn's text the term *Hinayana* is maintained over less pejorative terms such as *Theravada* (the name of the only surviving Hinayana school).

4. Mahayana teaching: Mahayana (Great Vehicle) teaches the Bodhisattva Way, which is the vow to practice for the sake of saving all beings from suffering. Bodhisattvas are beings who, through a deep vow of compassion, vow to put off their own entry into the tranquil extinction of Nirvana until the last being is saved from suffering. Its teachings can be said to begin with the Six Paramitas and to culminate in Zen. According to the Mahayana view, all phenomena may seem to exist; yet all phenomena are, at the same time, of the same substance, and therefore nonexistent in reality. Therefore the "impurity" that Hinayana teaching urges its followers to avoid is seen, in the Mahayana view, to be of the same interpenetrated reality as Nirvana itself: What could there then be to avoid? Hence comes the classically Mahayana view of fully interpenetrated "no hindrance," which is conclusively developed through the meditative insight of Zen.

5. Sudden Enlightenment: Teaches the dharma of seeing into one's nature and becoming a buddha in an instant, without having to progress through specific orders or stages of a particular path. It is in distinction to the Gradual Cultivation view, which posits that enlightenment is attained via stages, or striving through levels or degrees of insight and self-control, usually guided by precepts and forms of ethical conduct. The two approaches to enlightenment are often viewed as being opposite, even contradictory or incompatible. It is a debate that rages from time to time in the Mahayana and Zen schools. Master So Sahn shows, in *The Mirror of Zen*, the interplay of both Sudden Enlightenment and Gradual Cultivation in a student's practice.

6. The Complete Teaching: According to this dharma, all things do not hinder one another, and everything—whether living or lifeless—is originally buddha. Everything is interpenetrated. Be

it bright or dark, true or false, high or low, or large or small, everything is neither the same nor different. Its important scriptures are the *Avatamsaka Sutra* ("The Flower Ornament Sutra") and the *Lotus Sutra*.

7. Ananda: Literally, "joy" or "surprise." The name of the cousin of the Buddha and brother of Devadatta. It is said that Ananda was born on the night the Buddha attained enlightenment. He accompanied him as his personal attendant for some twenty-five years. He is regarded by tradition as one of the Ten Great Disciples of the Buddha. Renowned for his intelligence and extraordinary memory, Ananda is known as "foremost in hearing the Buddha's teachings." His extraordinarily faithful recollection of everything he heard in the Buddha's presence became the source of most, if not all, of the Buddhist scriptural canon when it was compiled shortly after the Buddha's death.

Chapter 6

1. Pao-chi (dates unknown): At one time the tutor to Emperor Wu of the Liang Dynasty. One day while Pao-chi was meditating, a funeral procession passed by his seat. Upon suddenly hearing one of the mourners wail in grief, he attained enlightenment.

2. Pao-shou Yen-chao (dates unknown): A senior monk once asked Pao-shou, "What was your Original Face before you were even born?" He became completely stuck, and could not answer. Many months of earnest practice still gave him no insight into the problem. One day, while he was walking in the market, he came upon a group of people engaged in a vicious fight. As the fight was broken up, one of the men muttered, "I have truly lost face today." Upon hearing these words, Pao-shou was immediately enlightened.

Chapter 10

1. *Hwa-du:* Literally "word-head," this term is often used interchangeably with *kung-an* (Kor.: *kong-an;* Jap.: *koan*), or "public case." It refers to some word, phrase, exchange, or situation whose seemingly obscure or doubtful meaning refines the meditation practitioner's own existential doubt, thus deepening his or her meditation. The word or phrase in itself is not important: rather, its function (which is a teaching technique unique to the Zen tradition) cuts off the way of discriminative thinking, leading the student to enlightenment.

2. Chao-chou Ts'ung-shen (778–897): One of the most influential and iconoclastic masters of the Zen tradition, he became a monk at a very early age. After arduous practice, he attained enlightenment and received Dharma transmission from Nan-ch'uan P'u-yuan, and continued to practice under his guidance for another twenty years. He passed away at the age of 120. One day, a monk asked Master Chao-chou, "What is the meaning of Bodhidharma's coming from the West?" This is another way of asking, "What is the meaning of the buddha-dharma? What is the Buddha's teaching?" Chao-chou replied, "The pine tree in the courtyard." The monk was instantly enlightened. This phrase is one of the classic dharma exchanges in the Zen tradition, and a *hwa-du* for many practitioners.

Chapter 11

1. Jumping out of the burning house: In the *Lotus Sutra,* the Buddha teaches that the unexamined life in this world of endless birth and death can be likened to children playing mindlessly within a burning house. Flames are devouring the building, but because we are habitually lost in self-amusement, we block any

self-insight into our condition: we are completely unaware of the extreme danger that at any moment may engulf us. The Buddha stated that a loving father would go to any lengths to draw his children out to safety. Yet if they still do not listen or follow, so absorbed in their inner attachments, he would even resort to "tricking" them into believing that gifts and presents awaited them on the outside, if only they would come out to get them. Appealing to their minds through the free use of no-hindrance expedient means that fit the situation, the Buddha compared his own use of teaching expedients to this kind of father. This is a very well-known allegory on expedient means.

Chapter 12

1. Live words/dead words: "Live words" are any words that point to reality as-it-is. "Dead words" are any words or speech based on mere intellection, ratiocination, or conceptual knowledge of any kind, even Buddhist.

2. Lin-chi (?–867): One of the great masters of the Zen tradition, his many students went on to found what became known as the Lin-Chi (Jap.: Rinzai) School. He became a monk at an early age and immediately began sutra study under a prominent master. After scriptural study, he practiced under the great Zen Master Huang-po Hsi-yun. He gave *inga* to twenty-two Dharma successors.

Chapter 13

1. Dog has no Buddha-nature: The Buddha taught that all things have Buddha-nature, which means that all beings can get enlightenment. To clear his doubt, a monk in China once asked Zen Master Chao-chou, "Does a dog have Buddha-nature?" Master Chao-chou instantly replied, "No!" Since then this dialogue

has become a central *hwa-du* for many Zen practitioners: "The Buddha taught that all things have Buddha-nature. Why did Chao-chou say that a dog has no Buddha-nature?" This is regarded as the "Mu!" *kong-an* (in Chinese, the single character *mu* means "no," "nothing," or "nothingness").

2. A monk approached the great Zen Master Tung-shan Liang-chieh (807–869) while he was weighing a bolt of flax, or hemp, used in the making of summer clothes. "Teacher, what is buddha?" he asked. Zen Master Tung-shan instantly replied, "Three pounds of flax!"

3. Zen Master Yun-men Wen-yen (862 or 864–949) had just finished relieving himself in the temple outhouse. A young monk entering the outhouse spontaneously asked him, "Master, what is buddha?" Master Yun-men replied, "Dry shit on a stick!" In temples in China, urine and feces were eliminated into wooden buckets inserted into an opening in the squatting-stalls. The wastes were then gathered at the end of the day for spreading into compost piles, and scooped out of the buckets with a long wooden paddle, or "shit stick." After cleaning, the stick—with any trace remainder of the day's wastes—was left hanging right outside the outhouse to dry in the sun, until the next day's work.

Chapter 14

1. Yung-chia Hsuan-chueh (665–713): He became a monk at the age of eight and began intensive study of the sutras. Initially trained in the special meditation practices of the T'ien-T'ai School, he was eventually awakened to his original nature while chanting the *Vimalakirti Sutra*. He was given *inga* by the Sixth Patriarch, and passed away at the age of forty-nine while seated in meditation.

2. Meng-shan Te-yi (dates unknown): A monk during the Yuan Dynasty.

Chapter 19

1. Six sense faculties: Eyes, ears, nose, tongue, body, mind. Faculties of sense through which function the six kinds of sense-consciousness (eye-consciousness, ear-consciousness, nose-consciousness, etc.) to grant apprehension of the six kinds of sense-objects (object of sight, object of hearing, object of smell, etc.).

2. Seeing a mourning son and hacking at his own leg: Once upon a time, a monk was seated in meditation out in the open air. A young man dressed in traditional mourning clothes and escorting a coffin came upon him and began screaming, "Why did you kill my mother? Why did you kill my mother?" After a contentious argument, the man produced a hatchet. Defending himself, the monk grabbed the hatchet, and in the ensuing struggle, looked down to see his own leg bleeding. Then he realized that the entire happening had merely been a moment of mental delusion!

Encountering a pig and grabbing his own nose: Once a monk, seated deep in meditation, was suddenly attacked by a wild boar. He grabbed desperately at the beast, grappling madly for a handhold, but was only able to latch on to the animal's nose. Clenching his hand tightly on the snout, the monk caused the boar to squeal madly. It was in this moment that the monk came to, screaming desperately, and realized that he had been grabbing his own nose during a moment of unclear meditation. These two examples are used to show the operation of Mara, or delusion, in a single moment of unclarity. In other words, the monks had made Mara in their own minds, and believed for a moment that it was real.

Chapter 22

1. Eight winds: The eight phenomena that can move the thinking mind: praise and censure, pleasure and suffering, prosperity and decline, honor and disgrace.

2. Kalpa: In classical Buddhist cosmology and metaphysics, an unimaginably long measure of time: it is regarded as pointless to attempt to enumerate it with numbers or words. This unfixed unit is sometimes expressed as the length of time it would take for a galaxy or world-system to come into being, remain, and cease to exist.

Chapter 26

1. Zen Master Wei-shan Ling-yu (771–853); Zen Master Yang-shan Hui-chi (803–887).

Chapter 27

1. The fifty-five stages of progress: According to the *Surangama Sutra*, in order to reach perfect buddhahood, the spiritual seeker passes through fifty-five measures, levels, or "stages" of progress: First, one must pass through the Land of Celestial Wisdom; then one must pass, stage by stage, through the Ten Kinds of Reliance, the Ten Abodes of Bodhisattvas, the Ten Practices, the Ten Kinds of Dedications to Bodhisattvas, the Four Paths of Endeavor, and, finally, the Ten Lands.

Chapter 31

1. Nirvana: Originally meaning "extinction, perfect quiescence, extinction of suffering as well as extinction of the way of extinction." Nirvana is a condition of utmost tranquillity and cessation, in which delusions neither appear nor disappear.

Chapter 33

1. The Five Precepts of Buddhism are I vow not to kill, I vow not to lie, I vow not to steal, I vow not to engage in unchaste conduct, and I vow not to take intoxicants. The last two are seen differently for lay practitioners than for monks and nuns, for whom they are regarded as more strictly binding.

Chapter 37

1. Manjushri Bodhisattva: In Mahayana Buddhism, the bodhisattva embodying wisdom who points to the original nature of mind. Often depicted holding a sword, which symbolizes the sword of wisdom that cuts through delusion, laying bare the unchanging nature of truth in all things, sometimes called "buddha."

2. Samantabhadra Bodhisattva: The bodhisattva-manifestation of vows and compassion. According to the *Avatamsaka Sutra*, Samantabhadra made the Ten Vows of a Bodhisattva. He depicts the practice and meditation of all the buddhas. In traditional iconography and thought, Samantabhadra is usually depicted, along with Manjushri, escorting Shakyamuni Buddha, forming together what is sometimes referred to as the "Shakyamuni trinity."

Chapter 38

1. The threefold practice: The Buddha urged upon his students the practice of *sila* (precepts), *samadhi* (meditation), and *prajna* (wisdom). The three practices do not follow in any linear order of study, nor are they to be practiced separate from one another. The Buddha taught that ethical conduct, meditation, and wisdom are the same practice with three different faces.

2. Six supernatural powers: Powers of perception, gained through meditation, which can enable us to grasp what cannot

normally be apprehended through the normal sense faculties:
(1) Power of the "spiritual leg": the ability to move anywhere
and to transform oneself at will; (2) power of the "spiritual eye":
the ability to see anything at any distance; (3) power of the
"spiritual ear": the ability to hear any sound at any distance; (4)
power of knowing others' minds: the ability to see the thoughts
of sentient beings; (5) power of knowing fate: the ability to perceive the former, present, and future lives of all sentient beings
who are cycling and recycling in the endless wheel of birth and
death in the six realms; (6) power of eradicating all illusions: the
ability to eliminate all afflictions.

The first five powers may be attained by those not practicing this buddha-dharma. There are examples such as yogis, sad-
dhus, Taoist hermits, and even disembodied spirits who practice
what Buddhist masters have called "impure" or "misdirected
samadhi," or intensive meditative practices. One can also achieve
such powers, however fleetingly, through mantra practices or even
special drugs. But any serious practitioner or teacher would not
consider this authentic insight.

The last power alone, however—the power of eliminating
afflictions through correct insight into the causes of the arising
of mind—can be attained by advanced practitioners of the
buddha-dharma: arhats (a perfected person, who has attained
Nirvana), bodhisattvas, and buddhas.

Chapter 39

1. Period of the decline of the Dharma: It is said that the
Buddha's teachings cannot help but be tainted as time passes
since Shakyamuni Buddha's death. This was declared by the
Buddha himself. According to this, there is a view of the history
of the buddha-dharma that posits a period of the true dharma,

the period of the derivative dharma, and the period of the decline of the dharma.

The first five hundred years following the death of Shakyamuni Buddha is regarded as the period of the true dharma, when the Buddha's teachings were circulated and practiced very much as when he was alive. Many people became serious practitioners, and a great many of these eventually attained enlightenment and achieved the holy fruit of Nirvana.

The next thousand years was the period of the derivative dharma. In many respects this is very much similar to the period of true dharma. During this time the Buddha's teachings were still being practiced more or less authentically. There were serious practitioners, but very few of them ever attained enlightenment.

The following 10,000-year period—the period in which Master So Sahn wrote this treatise, and which includes our own present era—is the period of the decline of the dharma. This is regarded as a time when the teachings, though substantially the same, begin to be weakened, watered down, diluted. Only a few real practitioners remain. Many false teachers appear. After the end of this 10,000-year period, the Buddha's teachings will be lost forever.

Yet such a periodization should not be taken as a standing rule. Practitioners who are conscious of history and who practice social justice are aware that the secular world is in a continual state of decline. When false things pretend to be true, that is the period of the decline of the dharma. On the contrary, when true things are revealed for their truth, it is the period of the true dharma. When we are blinded by the power of material culture and the easy life of the senses, and do not act with true compassion, this brings on the decline of the dharma. But if we are guided by the light of our self-nature and act according to the truth of things as they are, the period of the true dharma appears very clearly in front of us.

Chapter 40

1. The monk tied and bound with grasses: Once upon a time, a gang of highway robbers set upon a monk. Dragging him off the road into high grasses, the thieves took his begging bowl, his prayer beads, and even stripped him of his clothing. Then they bound his wrists and ankles with the grasses, pinning him firmly to the ground. They knew of the extreme nonviolence of Buddhist monks, so they reasoned that he would not tear up the grass to escape. And they were right. The monk was petrified of moving, fearing that any movement might tear up the grasses. He lay all day in the blazing sun and endured a long night of cold, yet still he would not tear up the grasses. Just then the king appeared, with a band of retainers, galloping through the field on a sporting hunt. Moved by the compassion of this begging monk who would not even harm a blade of grass to protect his own life, the king dismounted and untied the grasses himself. He was deeply moved by the monk, especially since he, the king, had only been out hunting animals for sport. And with this, the king converted to Buddhism.

2. The goose that swallowed a precious jewel: One day, while begging his alms from house to house, a monk came to the door of a villager who was also a prominent jeweler. The jeweler was at that time cutting a priceless gem at the behest of the king himself. When he stepped away from his low workbench for a few minutes, a goose that was wandering freely in the workshop leaned in and gobbled up the shiny stone. The jeweler returned to find the gem gone, and flew into a mighty rage. He naturally suspected the poor begging monk, and began to hurl such epithets

at the monk. But the monk said nothing, even though he had seen the goose gobble up the gem right before his eyes. He knew that if he revealed that the goose had eaten the gem, the goose would probably be killed on the spot. The jeweler grew even more incensed at the monk's silence, and eventually bound him and beat him with a stick, screaming that the gem must be returned if the monk wished to leave with his life. After hours of being accused, the monk noticed the goose excreting in the pen, and told the jeweler to look in the feces, where the gem was found.

Chapter 42

1. *Samadhi:* Taken in the strictest sense, this term refers to the highest meditative state that a human being can experience, a state of extraordinary calm and absolutely clear one-pointedness wherein no thoughts arise or disappear. However, Master So Sahn and others often use *samadhi* to refer simply to deep meditation, or one-pointed effort in meditation. Determining which of these senses is intended depends, here and elsewhere, on the context alone.

Chapter 45

1. Vimalakirti: The meaning in Sanskrit is "clear name" or "immaculate name." According to Mahayana tradition, specifically the sutra that bears his name, Vimalakirti was a lay devotee from Vaishali, in India, living at the time of the Buddha. He was known to be deeply enlightened, and so spiritually accomplished that even many of the Buddha's top students would not contend with him in debate. When he once fell ill, the Buddha sent many students to convey his concern and best wishes, led by the great Manjushri Bodhisattva, who was foremost among them in wisdom. An epic debate ensued, and on the question as

to "How would one express the experience of nonduality?" everyone's answers were deemed to be lacking. Manjushri stepped up
to answer, to great approval, "If you open your mouth to describe it, that's already not nondualism." Everyone was very im-
pressed, believing this to be the best answer. Then Vimalakirti
was asked the question, and he answered by remaining perfectly
silent. The assembly universally praised Vimalakirti for elucidat-
ing the dharma of nonduality most brilliantly. This scene is re-
counted in the *Vimalakirti Sutra*.

Chapter 46

1. *Dana*: In Buddhism, "voluntary giving to others" is a fundamental practice. For this reason it is listed as the first of the six
paramitas (see note 1 to chapter 48, below). There are three kinds
of giving: The first is the giving of material things to sentient beings that need them. The second is the giving of Dharma, which
is giving teachings that lead sentient beings to develop insight
into their own nature. And the third is to act together with sentient beings so as to lead them from ignorance and delusion to a
life of insight and compassionate action.

Chapter 48

1. The Six Paramitas: In the Mahayana tradition, a sixfold path
encompassing all of the major practices of Buddhism, by means
of which one can conduct an enlightened life and create an enlightened society. They are the *dana paramita* (generosity), the
sila paramita (morality, or conduct), the *kshanti paramita* (patience),
the *virya paramita* (diligence, perseverance, or energy), the *dhyana
paramita* (meditation), and the *prajna paramita* (wisdom). Like the
Threefold Practice (precepts, meditation, wisdom), this is not a
ladderlike or consecutive practice, and none of these practices

can be brought to any fruition without the others. A sutra says, "One *paramita* is all *paramitas*."

Chapter 49

1. "Never delude yourself!": The great Chinese Zen Master Wu-ye (762–823) would deliver this simple exhortation to any question directed at him.

Chapter 50

1. Mantra: The Sino-Korean can be translated as "true words," "holy words," "transcendent incantation." The term *mantra* means words that are true and nondelusional, a spiritual technique using sound and the repetition of sound to instill one-pointed focus or concentration in meditation, cutting off all discriminative thinking.

Chapter 52

1. NAMU AMITA BUL: Sino-Korean transliteration for "NAMU AMITA BUDDHA," which literally means "Veneration of Amita Buddha."

2. Fifth Patriarch of Zen: The Chinese monk Hung-jen (601–674) received Dharma transmission from the Fourth Patriarch Tao-hsin (580–651). Among his many disciples, Hui-neng (638–713) and Shin-hsiu (605–706) founded the southern "sudden enlightenment" school and the northern "gradual enlightenment" school of Zen, respectively. The Fifth Patriarch transmitted the Dharma to Hui-neng in 671 and passed away at the age of seventy-four.

3. Ten directions: The four cardinal points of the compass (north, south, east, and west), the four intermediate points of the

compass, and the zenith and nadir. It connotes the whole infinite universe.

4. Forty-Eight Vows: When Amita Buddha was practicing as Dharmakara Bodhisattva in a previous rebirth, he made a vow in the presence of the Universal Buddha that he himself would put off his own assumption of buddhahood until he had successfully striven to manifest forty-eight conditions for sentient beings. Due to aeons of strenuous practice, these vows were accomplished and he became Amita Buddha. *The forty-eight vows* is a term that refers to the heroic establishment of vows and wishes for sentient beings, as well as the diligent effort one makes in one's spiritual practice to gain such benefits for sentient beings.

5. Three divisions of time: The past, present, and future. It can also mean past, present, and future lives, though this usage is seen very rarely. Combined with "the ten directions," this phrasing is used to create for the student the sense of infinite time and infinite space, which ultimately means "no time, no space" in the sense that this chapter is offered.

6. Pure Land: A term for the Land of Utmost Bliss. For sentient beings tired of endless struggle in this mundane world, the Pure Land is depicted as a topographical reality toward which we can strive, but in fact it is actually just a trope describing the nature of mind when it is devoid of conceptual thinking. In the "Chapter on Buddha-lands" of the *Vimalakirti Sutra*, we hear "If one's mind is pure, the whole world is pure." And there is also the teaching, "If you become enlightened to your true nature, then even samsara is indeed the Pure Land."

7. Kuei-feng Tsung-mi (780–841): While reciting the *Sutra of Complete Enlightenment* at a religious service for a lay devotee, Kuei-feng was suddenly awakened to his true self. He later became

the Fifth Patriarch of the Hua-Yen School, and faithfully advocated the unity of meditation and scriptural study.

8. Asvaghosha (ca. 100–160): A Buddhist poet in India during the reign of King Kanishka of the Kushan Dynasty, he was by training a prominent Brahmin scholar and polemicist. He converted to Buddhism under the guidance of the Venerable Parsva and was revered as a living bodhisattva. He excelled in classical Sanskrit literature, and composed many sacred texts and treatises. One of his most important works, read to this day, is *Discourse on the Awakening of Faith in the Mahayana Way*.

9. Nagarjuna (ca. 150–250): Arguably one of the most influential Buddhist figures, other than the Buddha himself, Nagarjuna was born in southern India to a Brahman family. Originally a student of the Hinayana, he came to learn of the Mahayana from an old monk living in the Himalayas. Nagarjuna wrote voluminous commentaries on many Buddhist sutras and is credited with the development of the teaching that came to be known as the *Prajnaparamita Sutra*. He played a major role in the spread of Buddhist thought, and for this reason is often referred to as "the Second Buddha."

10. Hui-yuan (334–416): Educated in Confucianism and Taoism, he was awakened at the age of twenty-one when he heard a lecture on the *Prajnaparamita Sutra* given by the great Tao-an (314–385), and then joined the Buddhist monastic order. He is known for, among other things, establishing the White Lotus Society along with 123 other senior monks and devoted lay practitioners, dedicated to the practice of focused chanting as a means for awakening.

11. Jui-yen (dates unknown): A disciple of Master Yen-t'ou Ch'uan-huo (ca. 828–887), he was known for calling out to

himself—and answering himself—every single day: "Master?"
"Yes." "Keep a clear mind!" "Yes!" "Don't let yourself be deceived
by others—anytime, anyplace!" "Yes! Yes!!"

Chapter 53

1. Like eating a diamond: Quoted from the "Chapter on the
Coming of the Tathagata" in the *Avatamsaka Sutra*. If you eat a
diamond, it will not be broken down, digested, and turned to
waste. Rather, it will pass through the filthiness of your entrails
and appear again without having been tarnished or diminished
in the least. In the same way, if one makes even the smallest
karmic bond with the Buddhist teachings, this will not be diminished or wasted: It will eventually cut through one's filthy
delusion-world. The karma-body that suffers from ignorance
and its afflictions will be destroyed, and the highest stage of liberation made manifest.

2. Yung-ming Yen-shou (904–975): The Third Patriarch of
the Fa-Yen School as well as the Sixth Patriarch of the Pure
Land School. Among his many profound teachings, he is perhaps best known for the ardor of his daily practice: There were
108 specific daily practices to which he committed himself, and
he is known to have accomplished them every single day without fail. One of those practices, for example, was to chant the
sutras a certain large number of times every day. He communicated teachings by letter to the Korean King Gwang-Jong of
the Koryo Dynasty, and gave Dharma transmission to some
thirty-seven monks from Korea. As a result of his efforts, the Fa-
Yen School flourished in Koryo for quite some time.

Chapter 54

1. Kuei-feng Tsung-mi: See note 7, chapter 52.

Chapter 56

1. Children outside reenter the burning house: See note 1, chapter 11. Being tainted by the mundane world again after having cut off secular attachments to become a monk or nun would be as if the children in this *Lotus Sutra* episode were to reenter the burning house from which they have already escaped.

Chapter 57

1. The three worlds: In Sanskrit, *triloka*, sometimes translated as "three regions." The existence of sentient beings may be divided into three spiritual worlds: *kamaloka* (the world of desire), *rupaloka* (the world of form), and *arupaloka* (the world of formlessness). In the "world of desire," sentient beings possess desire for food, sex, wealth, sleep, and power. They are blindly attached to material things, and their minds are corrupt and coarsened thereby. The "world of form" is relatively brighter in spiritual condition, and sentient beings are less controlled by desire yet still prone to the power of anger. They are not completely free from matter. (*Form*, in the sense that it is used in these second two realms, essentially means the same as *matter*.) The "world of formlessness" is essentially the purest, since no material element (matter) exists, therefore desire and anger cannot exist. Still, beings stuck in this kind of world still retain the deluded notion of "I," so they cannot be said to be entirely free from all mental hindrance.

Many people will consider the "three worlds" to be a vertical or horizontal ordering of things, but this would be a mistaken view: they do not designate or inhabit any kind of physical space. Instead these terms refer to a kind of spiritual division of the mental world, namely the experiential world of *samatha* (insight). The "world of desire" is the sensuous and sensual realm; the "world of form" is a realm beyond the senses, yet still attached to the condition of form (matter); and the "world of formlessness" is a purely ideologic realm transcending all form (matter).

Needless to say, the three worlds are the realm in which we exist. And as such, they changefully manifest themselves in our minds to the degree to which we attach to the three poisons (desire, anger, and ignorance) in our minds.

Chapter 62

1. *The Record of the Transmission of the Lamp:* The original title is *The Record of the Transmission of the Lamp of Great Virtues*, in thirty volumes, compiled by the Sung Dynasty monk Tao-yuan in 1004. This collection records (some scholars believe, "creates") the lineages of Dharma transmission, declares the spiritual achievements, and notes the analects of some 1,701 masters of the fifty-two generations of the five Zen schools, ranging from the seven ancient Buddhas to the dharma successors of Fa-yen Wen-i. The 1,700 classic *kong-ans* were derived from this collection.

Chapter 63

1. *Maha Prajnaparamita Shastra:* Nagarjuna's extensive *Commentary on the Great Prajnaparamita* ("The Perfection of Wisdom in Twenty-Five Thousand Lines"). This text was translated into Chinese by the great Kumarajiva during the Eastern Jin Dynasty. Sanskrit and Pali originals do not survive.

Chapter 64:

1. *Brahamajala Sutra:* Its Sanskrit and Pali originals, too, do not survive. From this text we derive the so-called Bodhisattva Precepts, which comprise the Ten Great Precepts, which guard

against serious offenses, and the Forty-eight Precepts, which guard against lesser offenses. The Bodhisattva Precepts can be considered Mahayanist precepts—guidelines for ethical discipline based on the Mind-Ground teaching. The precepts in the *Brahamajala Sutra*, based as they are on the Mind-Ground teachings, do not belong to the classical *Vinaya* proper, but are regarded as highly as the teachings of the *Avatamsaka Sutra*.

Chapter 67

1. Three Evil Paths: Lower rebirths or spiritual conditions deemed the most wretched because those inhabiting them are the most seriously hindered in—if not denied—the path to enlightenment. Constituted by the animal realm, the realm of the hungry ghosts, and the hell realm. Although spoken of in terms of being possible conditions for rebirth, it would be wrong to consider them only as forms of life, forms that one takes after a physical death. Rather, the Buddha taught that these are spiritual states we risk many times every day: wandering with the trapped ignorance of an animal, wandering with insatiable hunger and thirst for things, and wandering in hellish mind-states.

Chapter 68

1. The *Sutra on Cause and Effect:* The original title is the *Sutra on Cause and Effect of Past and Present*, in four volumes, first translated into Chinese by the Tripitaka Master Gunabhadra (393–468) during the Liu-Song Dynasty. This sutra relates many stories of the Buddha's past lives. It emphasizes that every condition experienced in the present is but a direct reflection of conditions experienced or acted upon in the past.

2. The *Sutra on the Perfection of Wisdom in Seven Hundred Verses:* Otherwise known as the *Manjushri Sutra*, translated into Chinese

by Sanghapala (479–524) during the Liang Dynasty. It is a compendium of various precepts and lists the twenty-four kinds of
afflictions that develop and persist into becoming mind-habits.
It also enunciates the procedure for receiving the Bodhisattva
Precepts.

Chapter 72

1. *Sravaka:* "Voice-hearer." This term originally referred to
the disciples who heard Shakyamuni Buddha's words and teachings directly from him. Since then it has come to refer to a Buddhist monk or practitioner who, though practicing according to
the Buddha's teachings, only pursues his or her own liberation.
The Mahayana School, which lays primary stress on the great
vow to save all sentient beings from suffering, frequently makes
light of the voice-hearers, ridiculing them, too, as progenitors
of a narrow spiritual direction, even selfishness, in their efforts.

2. Two Vehicles: The path of the *sravakas* ("voice-hearers")
and *pratyeka-buddhas* (solitary practitioners).

Chapter 73

1. Five Skandhas: *Skandha* is the Sanskrit term for "aggre-
gate," "cluster," or "bunch." A very key concept in Mahayana
teachings, the five skandhas are *form, feelings, perceptions, impulses*
(mental formations, or karma), and *consciousness.* Form connotes
all material elements, or the matter-realm. Feelings refer to sen-
sations evoked by outside stimuli. Perceptions are any concep-
tualization of the forms of outside things. Impulses constitute
all that we might term psychological operations not derived
from feelings or perceptions, and represent the operation of the
will in particular. Finally, consciousness is the pure mental activity that synthesizes all mental operations.

The concept of the five *skandhas* helps to explain the constitution of the existence-world, and specifically the existence of the human's *being*. What some people call the Buddhist "denial" of the self—"no-self"—is actually an experiential statement, coming out of direct insight, that the human's being is the mere result of the temporary dependent origination of subject and object: a transcendental self or its purported substantial identity does not autonomously exist.

In sum, the five *skandhas* are a general term describing all material elements and fleeting mental operations that, operating together, we mistakenly take to be a "self." They are all illusions created by deluded thinking. In reality, the stuff we take to be a "self" or "a being" is actually just a loosely aggregated cluster of flickering causes and conditions, fleetingly bundled together, always changing, and having no independent, self-arising nature of its own. Having insight into the emptiness of the five *skandhas*, according to Buddhist teaching, grants the practitioner liberation from all the suffering and distress that we ascribe to the purported existence of this illusory "I."

2. Only in old age and in fear of death, people resort to the Buddha!: Adapted from the writings of Shao-yong (1011–1077), the highly esteemed I Ching master, Confucian sage, Taoist adept, and humble philosopher who greatly influenced the development of the Idealist school of Neo-Confucianism during the Sung Dynasty. He called himself "Mr. Happiness," and his rude, rustic dwelling, "the Happy Nest." His exact words were, "People devotedly follow Confucius when they are young and striving after prestige and wealth. Only in their old age, and in fear of death, do they finally resort to the Buddha!" Though Confucian, he introduced key Buddhist teachings into his philosophy. Master So Sahn's easy familiarity with this quote reveals that he

was quite conversant with the intellectual currents surrounding his Buddhist tradition.

Chapter 74

1. Pai-yun Shou-tuan (1025–1072): Received Dharma transmission from Zen Master Yang-ch'i Fang-hui.

Chapter 75

1. Yun-men Wen-yen (862 or 864–949): See note 3, chapter 13. One of the towering masters of the entire Zen tradition. Born in Zhejiang Province, Yun-men became a monk at an early age, and began his study in the Vinaya (Precepts) School. After experiencing an awakening when his leg was broken as he was being driven from the temple by one master, he deepened his study under the guidance of Zen Master Hsueh-feng I-ts'un. He eventually attained perfect enlightenment, and became his Dharma successor. He continued to spread the Dharma for many years at Mount Yun Men, hence the name by which we know him today. He had eighty-eight Dharma successors.

Chapter 76

1. A sudden shout of "HO!" [transliterated as "HAL!" in Korean, while in Japanese, transliterated as "KATZ!" or "KATSU!"]: A loud, thundering cry intended to cut off discriminating thinking and return the one who hears it to just-this, right-now mind. Pointing to substance, an expedient means without words, cutting through the student's conceptual thinking in a flash. According to popular belief, it was Zen Master Ma-tsu (see note 1, chapter 78) who first employed this technique to shatter his students' conceptions. It is recorded that the great Pai-chang, when he first experienced his teacher Ma-tsu's thunderous shout, went

deaf for three days. Many Zen teachers have taken to using this singular teaching tool, with Zen Master Lin-chi (?–867) perhaps most notable in this regard. Similarly, Zen Master Te-shan would pound a student with his large Zen stick whenever he was asked a question, while Zen Master Chu-chih (dates unknown) would wordlessly raise one finger.

Chapter 77

1. Zen Master Tung-shan Liang-chieh (807–868).

Chapter 78

1. Ma-tsu Tao-i (709–788): One of the loftiest peaks in the Zen world, he became a monk at a young age. He quickly stood out as one of the most diligent practitioners in the community of Zen Master Huai-jang at Mount Nan Yueh. Venerable Tao-i was known to out-sit even the most diligent of meditators, going off by himself to continue his sitting long after the rest of the community had turned in for sleep. But his teacher saw then that even this intrepid ardor had a little problem. . . . One day Huai-jang sought out Tao-i, who was sitting out in an open space. "What are you doing?" he asked the young monk, who was sitting bolt upright on his mat.

"Why, I'm sitting meditation, sir."

"And what on earth are you sitting meditation for?"

"To become a buddha," Tao-i replied. Whereupon the Master walked off, and in a few minutes Tao-i was startled by a jarring, grating sound. Looking up, he saw his teacher grinding two ceramic roof tiles together. "What are you grinding those tiles together for?" he asked.

"I'm trying to make a mirror," the Zen master replied.

"But that's preposterous," Tao-i said. "Anyone knows you cannot make a mirror like that!"

"And so with you. Do you think you can 'become a buddha' by just sitting there like that?" The young Tao-i was immediately awakened.

"Teacher, how should I practice, then?"

Zen Master Huai-jang replied, "If a cart drawn by an ox refuses to move, is it appropriate to whip the cart or the ox?"

"Why, the ox, of course."

"In the same way, true Zen is not just about body-sitting; Zen is mind-sitting. It is not about refusing to lie down to sleep, and no one became a buddha just by sitting still for long periods. Zen is no-attachment, with nothing to achieve or abandon." At that moment Tao-i attained complete enlightenment, and later received Dharma transmission from Huai-jang. He produced some 139 Dharma successors. Many of his students also transmitted the Dharma to Korean monks of the Shilla Dynasty who traveled to China for practice.

2. Pai-chang Huai-hai (720 or 749–814): Initially studied sutras under Master Ma-tsu, and attended him closely. After attaining enlightenment at Zen Master Ma-tsu's deafening shout, Pai-chang received transmission and gathered a large community under his tutelage. Until that time, Zen centers in China had traditionally followed the monastic system stipulated in the *Vinaya Pitaka*. Pai-chang established a unique system of communal living. He made regulations and established a newer economic foundation that reflected the cultural and temporal spirit of the time in China. Ever since, the "Holy Rules of Pai-chang" have exerted enormous influence on how every subsequent Zen monastery has organized its communities. One of his most well

known maxims for life in the Zen school is "A day without work is a day without eating."

3. Huang-po Hsi-yun (?–850): A child prodigy, he entered the monastery at Mount Huang Po in Jiangxi Province. He asked his teacher, Pai-chang, how he had gotten enlightenment under Ma-tsu. Master Pai-chang replied, "At Master Ma-tsu's 'HO!!' I became totally deaf—I couldn't hear for three whole days!" At this, Huang-po's jaw dropped in amazement and, it is said, his tongue fell out to his chin. He was completely enlightened. This is the meaning of Ma-tsu's shout extending all the way down through his student, and so even "making Huang-po's tongue hang down from his mouth." Huang-po is one of the greatest figures in Zen, not least because he produced the iconoclastic Zen Master Lin-chi, First Patriarch of the Lin-Chi School.

Chapter 79

1. According to Charles Mark Mueller, a scholar of Korean Buddhism, "Ching-shan Tsung-kao was a very famous master but he was not the legitimate successor of Yuan-wu K'o-chin. The legitimate successor is Hu-ch'in Shao-lung." Quoted in footnote 126, "The Mirror of Zen" (Seoul, 1991: Propagation Department of the Chogye Order of Korean Buddhism), from the official website of the Chogye Order (www.koreanbuddhism .org), page N.A.

Chapter 80

1. Charles Mark Mueller again adds an important footnote here: "[The Sixth Patriarch] Hui-neng is said to have put a stop to the transmission of the robe and the bowl [which traditionally authenticated transmission]. The robe and bowl purportedly

were passed down from the time of the Buddha in a single line of succession. Hui-neng's discontinuation of the tradition allowed the transmission to branch out into many lineages, each one tracing itself back through Hui-neng to the Buddha. By Master So Sahn's time, most of those in the Korean Zen tradition traced their lineage through the Korean Zen Master T'aego, who had received transmission from a Chinese master of the Lin-chi lineage. Many Korean Zen adherents considered the Lin-chi lineage to be purer; hence, they referred to the other lineages as 'peripheral transmissions'" (Ibid., footnote 127). It is unclear from whom, exactly, Master T'aego (1301–1382)—and hence, the Korean Zen lineage that descends from him—received authentic transmission, other than some unnamed "Chinese master of the Lin-chi lineage."

Chapter 85

1. Tan-hsia burning a wooden image of the Buddha: One particularly cold winter day, the Zen Master Tan-hsia Tien-jan (?–1119) took up residence in an old temple. The temple was poor and rundown; there was hardly any food to eat, and no wood to cut for heating. So Master Tan-hsia entered the Main Buddha Hall and removed the wooden buddha statue from the altar, carried it outside, and began to light it on fire. As the flames grew and he warmed his hands over the heat, another monk came running up to him.

"Are you out of your mind? How dare you use the buddha for firewood!"

"Firewood?" Master Tan-hsia replied, nonplussed. "I'm not using this buddha for firewood. I'm only trying to burn some relics out of it." (According to Buddhist traditions, crystallized relics appear after the cremation of especially holy monks, saints, and buddhas.)

"That's nonsense! How can you get relics from a piece of wood?"

"Well, then," Tan-hsia responded. "If it's only wood, then why shouldn't we let it warm us?" And with this, he tossed more kindling on the fire, rubbing his hands over it.

2. Feeding the Buddha to a hungry dog: According to tradition, when Shakyamuni Buddha was born, he took seven steps and, pointing directly up to the sky with one hand and to the ground with his other hand, said, "In all the heavens above, and all the lands below, only 'I' is holy." Many years later Zen Master Yun-men (see also note 1, chapter 75) famously commented, "If I had been there when the Buddha did that, I would have killed him with one blow and thrown his corpse to a hungry dog. Then there would really be world peace!"

3. The old lady's refusal to meet the Buddha: [Source material undetermined.]

About the Editor

Hyon Gak Sunim, a Zen monk, was born Paul Muenzen in Rahway, New Jersey. Educated at Yale College and Harvard University, he was ordained a monk under Zen Master Seung Sahn in 1992 at Nam Hwa Sah Temple, the temple of the Sixth Patriarch, Guangzhou, People's Republic of China. He has completed more than twenty intensive ninety-day meditation retreats and three arduous hundred-day solo meditation retreats in the mountains of Korea. He has compiled and edited a number of Zen Master Seung Sahn's texts, including *The Compass of Zen, Only Don't Know,* and *Wanting Enlightenment Is a Big Mistake*. He received *inga* from Zen Master Seung Sahn in 2001, and is currently guiding teacher of the Seoul International Zen Center at Hwa Gye Sah Temple, Seoul. Hyon Gak Sunim can be contacted via e-mail at hyongak@yahoo.com.